Greatness in Construction History

Greatness in Construction History

*Human Stories of Great People
and Great Projects*

Dr. Sherif Hashem

Leader in applied, concise business books

First published in 2022 by
Business Expert Press, LLC
222 East 46th Street, New York, NY 10017
www.businessexpertpress.com

ISBN-13: 978-1-94709-804-6 (paperback)
ISBN-13: 978-1-94709-805-3 (e-book)

Business Expert Press Portfolio and Project Management Collection

First edition: 2022

10 9 8 7 6 5 4 3 2 1

Description

This book takes the reader on a journey through times and spaces to live the stories and glories of some eight great projects shaping the world's skyline. It uncovers the secrets of construction greatness through living the project stories firsthand, meeting with the great builders and world leaders behind the projects.

The reader will witness the merger of souls into bodies of the newborn buildings, live their lives, and sometimes their death or suicide. The journey begins with the pyramids of ancient history, on to the magic of the middle ages, to the passion of the renaissance era, down to the industrial revolution, and modern ages. The book contains PMBOK® Guide, Agile, and Design–Build project management reviews, hence good for both project managers and construction history fans, alike. Enjoy!

Keywords

project management; construction management; construction history; project stories; greatness; construction; PMBOK® Guide; PMI; leadership; Agile; design–build; step pyramid; florence dome; brooklyn bridge; eiffel tower; empire state building; al gourna village; crystal palace; taj mahal; lessons learned; love stories; renaissance; the power of design–build

Contents

Acknowledgments

All praise is due to Allah, the Lord of the Worlds

"He initiated you from the earth, and He settled you on it."

Quran 11:61

Acknowledgment, credit, and respect go to the noble known or unknown people who lost or spent their lives on construction sites to achieve construction greatness.

As such, if this book was given another name, it would have certainly been

"The Martyrs of Construction Greatness."

I would like to thank my dear wife, Jwan Salman, for being there for me each step of the way, and for offering brilliant ideas and contributions until the book came to life.

I would like to thank my dear sons Omar Hashem, Ahmed Hashem, and Karim Hashem for giving me reasons to live and shine in my career as a professional and a writer.

I would like to thank Dr. Tim Kloppenborg for his wonderful support and inspiration, and Mr. Scott Isenberg of BEP for his outstanding leadership and for believing in me.

Finally, special thanks go to my dear mother the banker Hoda Hanem Ahmed Zeineldin (RIP), and my dear father the lawyer Fouad Fawzy Mohamed Hashem (RIP) for bringing me up in an environment that hails the values of faith, philanthropy, knowledge, fairness, and justice.

CHAPTER 1

The Pathway to Construction Greatness

Construction greatness means no less than making history.

It takes vision, novelty, geniality, persistence, and courage to get there. The spirit of construction greatness is unmistakable. When it happens you feel it, and when you live its glorious stories firsthand, your life will change forever. Out of the millions of buildings in the world, only a few are known by name or looks, the rest are just numbers. The difference is in greatness.

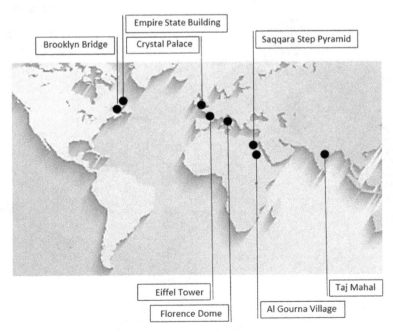

Figure 1.1 Great projects location map

Table of Contents

Preface

Great projects require great project management. They have their own trade secrets, common traits, and attributes. The term "project management" is a modern term that only came to life in the 20th century. However, the project management process itself is as old as the first construction effort on earth. In a look at construction history, great construction leaders tend to think of themselves as profession bests, history makers, builders of civilization, rather than just project managers. They create the conditions and right platform for construction greatness. And, in doing that, they had their own trade secrets. The pathway to construction greatness, however, can still be traced by taking a journey through times and spaces. Back in time and space to where and when great projects took place and live their stories firsthand. That includes being there before the projects started, living the environment that led to greatness, meeting with the great people who made greatness happen, and living the project events and proceedings from inception to completion. In doing that, secrets of construction greatness can be deciphered, invaluable life and project management lessons learned, and the pathway to construction greatness charted for future generations. This book takes the reader on such a journey through times and spaces, living the stories of eight great ancient projects that are still shaping the world skyline today, as shown in Figure 1.1. The journey is astonishing and the stories are inspiring and full of life wisdom and project management lessons.

1.1 My Journey Through Time and Space

Greatness in construction has its own secrets and conditions precedent. These need to be discovered and learned so that we can carry the torch and take the industry further. This is what this book is all about, to connect the current generation of engineers, architects, and construction history fans to their ancestors of great builders who made history through landmark constructions. To that end, I had to take a journey through time and space, back to when and where the great ancient buildings shaping the world's skyline took place. The idea was to live the project stories firsthand and meet with the people who built them. The driving force was my belief in the need to learn from such projects, and the outcome would be this book. A long list of candidate great buildings rushed to my mind, so I had to develop a selection criteria. The premise was that construction greatness is measured by impact. That means, a great building is necessarily famous, fascinating, and passed the test of time in terms of fame and impression. I made up my mind fast, and then came the question of where to start. To that end, the decision was to dig into construction history and find the first documented construction project ever. That turned out to be Imhotep's 2650 BCE Step Pyramid in Ancient Egypt. So the journey began and the beginning was so inspiring. The journey then continued in a free and instinctive manner all over the world map and back and forth in time. The second trip was onward to 1929 AD in New York to live the glory of the Empire State Building. The third trip was backward in time to 1420 AD in Italy to live the dawn of the Renaissance's era in Florence and Florence Dome or the il Duomo. The fourth trip was onward to 1880 AD in France to enjoy the story of art and science and the iron lady symbol of love, the Eiffel Tower. The fifth trip took me home to 1946 AD in Upper Egypt to join the making of Al Gourna Mud Palaces, the architecture of the poor. The sixth trip was once again to New York in 1867 AD to join the Roeblings' family in designing and building my favorite structural landmark, the Brooklyn Bridge. The seventh trip was a little further backward in time to 1850 AD in London to live the story of the thrill and glory of the ghost that appeared and vanished twice, the great Crystal Palace (RIP). At this point I got really exhausted, after a long journey covering seven projects and ca 5,000 years. However, three more buildings remained in my mind, of which one I felt the journey wouldn't be complete without it, the great Taj Mahal mausoleum. So, I gathered a pulse of energy and flew on to 1631 AD in Agra/India, attracted by the magic and majesty of the eternal mausoleum of Taj Mahal, the tear on the face of eternity. I lived the great project story, and that was where the journey came to a fulfilling end.

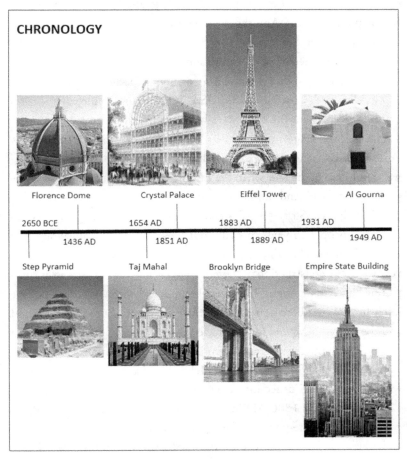

Figure 1.2 Great projects chronology

The following paragraphs summarize the backgrounds and beginnings of the journey's eight great project stories, shown in Figure 1.2, casting light on individual project settings and conditions precedence required for construction greatness to come to life and blossom.

Great Project Story #1—Pharaoh Djoser's Step Pyramid at Saqqara Necropolis, Ancient Egypt—The Wonder of Imhotep, the Architect who became a Mythical God: It's 2670 BCE in the deserts of Memphis, ancient Egypt. The young and powerful pharaoh Djoser accesses the throne, full of energy and determination to make history. Imperial resources were vast, and so were the ambitions of the new pharaoh. Djoser's first goal was having a pathway to heaven. He picked his genius vizier and polymath Imhotep for that task. And the story began.

Great Project Story #2—The Empire State Building, New York, USA—The Winner of NYC Skyscrapers "Race into the Sky" speeding 444-m height in 444 days' time. The Wonder of John Raskob: It's 1929 AD in New York City, New York, USA. While plans for the construction of the Empire State Building were being finalized, a fierce competition erupts over the title of the "World's Tallest Building," and a major New York Stock Exchange (NYSE) crash hits the economy. Chrysler Building was about to win the race when the Empire State Building gets in to make a spectacular win. And the story began.

Great Project Story #3—Florence Dome, Florence, Italy—il Duomo that took people 53 years to figure out how to build it. The Wonder of Filippo Brunelleschi: It's 1420 AD in Renaissance Florence, Italy. It's the year when the construction of Florence Dome started, 53 years after completing the dome design. The secret behind such delay was that no one knew how to build the dome. Renaissance architects waited for a method and the cathedral waited for a miracle. This is when Filippo Brunelleschi came up with the method and the miracle. And the story began.

Great Project Story #4—The Eiffel Tower, Paris, France—The Iron-work Monster that turned into a Symbol of Love. The Wonder of Gustave Eiffel: It's the mid-1880 AD in Paris, France. France is getting ready to celebrate the first centennial of its great revolution. The celebration had to be great and planned to host the 1889 AD World Fair. The World Fair monument had to be great. As great as France's history, and as high as France's profile and ambitions. That was the Eiffel Tower. And the story began.

Great Project Story #5—New Al Gourna Village, Luxor, Egypt—The Story of the Doomed Domed Mud Palaces. The Wonder of Architect Hassan Fathy: It's 1946 AD in Luxor, Egypt. A royal decree to relocate Al

Gourna village resting atop a pharaonic necropolis. Hassan Fathy takes over the mission and builds a great green village. The universe loved the new village, and the nature celebrated the birth of Green Architecture. All good and fine, however, a big surprise was waiting for Hasan Fathy. And the story began.

Great Project Story #6—The Brooklyn Bridge, New York, USA—Story of the Eighth Wonder of the World and the Martyrs of Construction Greatness. The Wonder of the Three Great Roeblings: It's 1867 AD in New York City, New York, USA. Immigrants pouring into New York City, mostly working in Manhattan and living in Brooklyn City. The two cities are growing fast; however, growth is restrained by the water body separating them, the East River. New York State steps in and appoints John A. Roebling to close the gap with a suspension bridge. And the story began.

Great Project Story #7—The Crystal Palace, London, UK—The Royal Ghost that appeared twice before vanishing in the flames. The Wonder of Joseph Paxton: It's 1850 AD in London, England, UK. The world is having a new beginning after the first Industrial Revolution. A new world of gears and machines. The British Queen invites the world to celebrate the glorious moment. Celebration had to be great, the moment had to glitter, and modernity had to glimmer. That's when the great Crystal Palace appeared on the horizon. And the story began.

Great Project Story #8—Taj Mahal Mausoleum, Agra, India—The Teardrop on the Face of Eternity—The Wonder of Ustad Ahmad Lahouri: It's 1631 AD in Agra, Uttar Pradesh, India. The Mughal Emperor Shah Jahan loses his beloved wife Empress Mumtaz Mahal. The heartbroken widower falls into deep remorse, then decides to turn his eternal love into an eternal mausoleum. The mausoleum had to reflect the greatness of his love and the unrivaled beauty of his adored wife. And the story began.

The journey through time and space was full of excitement. Whereas each project story had its own heroes, excitements, and outcomes, all projects had a shared wisdom and outcome. That is, "construction is human." Great buildings are not just steel and stone, but they have souls, memories, and feelings. After all, all buildings are built by humans for humans, with all what comes therewith from human emotions, ambitions, persistence, patience, joy, anger, and at times sorrow and pain. That is how great buildings engrave themselves in people's minds and hearts, and that's when the fun of reading great stories dwells.

1.2 The Timeless Domains of Construction Project Management

Certainly, and as proven through the ages, construction project management is not as simple as it might appear. In fact, it is an inherently complicated process involving numerous activities with numerous risks, unknowns, interdependencies, and requires numerous timely decisions each step of the way. However, whether intentionally or not, and no matter whether projects are modern or ancient, project delivery involves two obvious interactive tracks running along the project life span. These are the Technical track and the Project Management track. The Technical track domain is concerned with design, engineering, construction, and innovation, whereas the Project Management track domain is concerned with funding, planning, procurement, and governance. The Project Management track starts the process upon contract award by the owner with a go signal to the Technical track. The Technical track responds with design and construction information feeding procurement. The Project Management track responds by initiating the procurement process, so the project starts to progress. When any part of the project is completed, the Technical domain informs the Project Management domain for control and validation. The exchange of signals between the Project Management and Technical tracks repeats and continues causing the project to zigzag its way forward. With time, the project progresses incrementally toward completion and acceptance by the owner. In great projects, the Technical and the Project Management tracks collaborate and interact in creative ways that make projects stand out and cause construction greatness to exist. This dynamic interactive process is depicted in Figure 1.3 with focusing on the zigzagging between the Technical and Project Management domains. In reality, the Project Management role can be played by a project manager, project sponsor, or a contracting agency. The Technical role can be played by a design manager, construction manager, or a master builder. Indeed, in ancient times, master builders took the lead on both technical and project management tracks, however invariably under a sort of oversight by a higher authority representing the project owner. The master builder model is currently being replaced by modern design–build entities taking responsibility of all aspects of the design engineering, procurement, and construction activities. That is in lieu of the prevailing traditional design–bid–build approach involving a problematic separation between designers and builders. The design–build project delivery route changes and simplifies such approach. It involves appointing a single design–build entity to design and construct the works through a single design–build contract stating project scope and providing a high-level conceptual design and project-specific requirements of the owner [1].

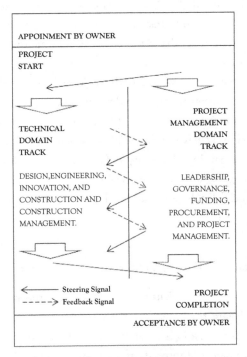

Figure 1.3 The interaction between project management and technical tracks

As from the dawn of history until recent times, construction project management used to be done without a documented project management approach. Instead, it heavily depended on the ingenuity of the master builders who used instinct, talent, expertise, and trade secrets, without proper documentation. It's only in the beginning of the 20th century that project management tools and techniques started to develop and become known. To highlight is the groundbreaking Scientific Management theory developed by Frederick Winslow Taylor in 1911 AD, also known as Taylorism. The theory focused on applying science to the manufacturing process and using workflows to control the work and improve productivity. Traces of Scientific Management can still be found in today's modern project management in terms such as analysis, efficiency, and standardization of best practices. Taylorism prompted a worldwide spread of project management appreciation and popularity. That was manifested in the establishment of the Project Management Institute PA/USA in 1969 AD, the Design–Build Institute of America DC/USA in 1993 AD, in addition to numerous other American and international project management groups, associations, and educational programs. Today, project management possesses a massive body of knowledge, and became the name of the game when it comes to developing construction projects or delivering organizational objectives. In the next years, project management is expected to achieve exponential growth and development, thanks to the new trends gaining popularity so fast such as Building Information Modeling (BIM), Agile project management, 3D printing, Lean Construction, Artificial Intelligence, all on the back of the superfast growing digital and IT sector.

1.3 The Axiomatic Trios of Construction Greatness

Great projects, whether ancient or modern, follow the same underlying principles and share the same common objectives and ultimate goals. The basics are timeless, and the objectives are almost identical. That concept would be easier to appreciate if we know that people haven't really changed significantly over the ages. The mentality is very similar and the motivations and human nature remained surprisingly repeating itself. The desire to achieve construction greatness has been happening throughout the history of the world wherever humans existed with the same DNA. Despite the vast differences in times and spaces between projects, construction greatness had always maintained certain common inherent traits, challenges, and outcomes. The basic traits required to deliver great projects remained valid, shining, transferrable, and decisive. The set of rules and principles of greatness always paused themselves wherever great construction existed or wanted to exist. These rules and objectives would be called self-evident realities, or just Axioms. These include a number of Axiomatic Trios. One of the most famous Axiomatic Trios is that of people, process, and technology. Another is the project management Axiomatic Trio of time, cost, and quality. However, the ultimate construction greatness Axiomatic Trio would be that identified by the Roman Architect Vitruvius Polio in the first-century BCE, namely, the trio of Firmness, Commodity, and Delight, as shown in Figure 1.4.

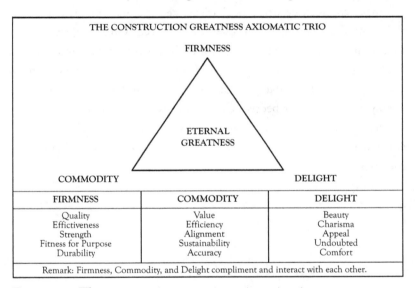

THE CONSTRUCTION GREATNESS AXIOMATIC TRIO

FIRMNESS

ETERNAL GREATNESS

COMMODITY   DELIGHT

FIRMNESS	COMMODITY	DELIGHT
Quality	Value	Beauty
Effectiveness	Efficiency	Charisma
Strength	Alignment	Appeal
Fitness for Purpose	Sustainability	Undoubted
Durability	Accuracy	Comfort

Remark: Firmness, Commodity, and Delight compliment and interact with each other.

Figure 1.4 The construction greatness axiomatic trio

Great projects must have great quality, great value, and great design. These requirements are achieved through the Axiomatic Trio of Firmness, Commodity, and Delight, respectively. All for a very long time spanning nations and generations.

Firmness, corresponds to the modern term Quality, and means that great buildings must have enough strength to withstand their self-weight and the forces of their users and of the nature for its intended life span. A building needs to stand up, keep its users dry and warm in the winter and cool in the summer. It must shed water away from its structure to prevent rot in organic materials, decay in masonry, and corrosion in metals.

Commodity, corresponds to the modern term Value, and means that great buildings must be designed and laid out effectively and efficiently so that the spaces for related activities are adjacent. They must be aligned accurately both in plans and in sections for their levels and spaces. Construction materials must be used efficiently, and the most appropriate materials specified for each element of the building in terms of sustainability and durability.

And, Delight, corresponds to the modern term Design, which simply means comfort, beauty, and charisma. These qualities might be regarded as subjective and resting in the eye of the beholder. However, in construction greatness, comfort, beauty, and charisma become unanimous, thanks to the talent and secrets mastered by great Architects. Great projects appeal to most people and keep people gazing at them with pleasure and respect.

Conclusion of the journey and the book is that construction greatness is a rare commodity. That goes for both ancient and modern times. It is simply as rare as great people. Great projects cannot be copied, cannot be challenged, and are eternal in people's minds. The top ten secrets of construction greatness are listed in the last page of the last Chapter of the book.

Enjoy!

CHAPTER 2

The Step Pyramid of Djoser, Memphis, Egypt—Imhotep and the Pharaoh's Stairway to Heaven

It's 2670 BCE in the deserts of Memphis, Egypt.

The young and powerful pharaoh Djoser accesses the throne, full of energy and determination to make history. Imperial resources were huge, and so were the ambitions of the new pharaoh. Djoser's first goal was building a pathway to heaven. He picked his genius vizier and polymath Imhotep for such impossible feat, and the story begins.

Figure 2.1 The Step Pyramid of Pharaoh Djoser—Memphis, Egypt [1]

Table of Contents

Preface

Greatness in construction requires a can-do attitude. When the task seems impossible, question the status quo, activate your inner powers, and think out of the box. That's the case in the story of the eternal Pharaoh Djoser's Step Pyramid. The task was a pathway to heaven. The status quo was mudbrick construction. The future was made of stone. Imhotep, the genius architect and polymath, then got creative and summoned innovation. As a result, greatness occurred. Imhotep carved his name in history by challenging the status quo and activating the power of innovation. The power of daring to adopt new building concepts and engineering materials simply, effectively, and confidently. The kind of power that's only available to great minds and great builders who can make history and know-how buildings work. Going for a traditional mudbrick royal tomb similar to those prevailing in Saqqara Necropolis at the time was just not an option. It neither lived up to the passion of the genius architect nor to the ambition of the powerful pharaoh. Imhotep set free his knowledge, skills, and talents. The outcome was an unprecedented Step Pyramid reaching the heavens of the skies. A monument that had marked the start of the Old Kingdom Third Dynasty, and is still standing with dignity 47 centuries after its construction defying age, winds, weather, earthquakes, and wars.

What Makes This Project Great

Pharaoh Djoser's Step Pyramid, shown earlier in Figure 2.1, marks the start of the Stone Age and stone buildings in the history of building construction. Moreover, the following 10 points explain why Pharaoh Djoser's Step Pyramid is great by any measure or standard:

1. The first major stone structure in the history of construction.
2. The highest man-made building in the world at the time of its construction.
3. Paved the way for the construction of the Great Pyramids of Giza, which were built ca 100 years later.
4. Its Architect Imhotep was worshiped by ancient Egyptians soon after his death and raised to a mythical demigod.
5. The pyramid's innovative step shape introduced a fundamental departure from previous tomb architecture.
6. The first documented integrated Design–Build project in the history of building construction.
7. The first sustainable project in history having used natural building stones from a nearby on-site trench.
8. Despite deterioration, it is the oldest monument in the world still standing for ca 4,700 years.
9. The first pharaonic tomb to include a major underground maze of tunnels and galleries.
10. The first documented project to utilize spiritual project management.

Story Starring and Key Characters

This story is starred by all project participants, in particular, the great unknown laborers and their families without their contribution greatness would not have been achieved.

Table 2.1 Story starring and key characters

Khasekhemwy [2]	Name	Pharaoh Khasekhemwy
	Meaning	The two powerful ones appear
	Title	Last Pharaoh of the Second Dynasty of Egypt
	Legacy	Reunited Upper and Lower Egypt after a fierce civil war between the followers of the ancient Egyptian gods Horus and Seth. Paved the way to the Old Kingdom great era in the Third Dynasty.
	PM Role	Undefined—died before the project started.
Djoser [3]	Name	Pharaoh Djoser
	Meaning	The divine of body
	Title	First Pharaoh of the Third Dynasty of Egypt
	Legacy	Founder of the Third Dynasty and the Old Kingdom, led an era of stability and renaissance, ordered the construction of the legendary Djoser's Step Pyramid at Saqqara.
	PM Role	Project Sponsor
Imhotep [4]	Name	Imhotep
	Meaning	The one who comes in peace
	Title	Vizier and Chancellor of Pharaoh Djoser
	Legacy	The first architect in history, polymath, highest priest of Ptah, and Master Builder of Pharaoh Djoser's Step Pyramid, and a perceived mythical demigod of medicine and healing.
	PM Role	Project Manager

Pharaoh Khasekhemwy, who reigned from 2690 to 2670 BCE, is the last pharaoh of the Second Dynasty of ancient Egypt. He made history by uniting Egypt's upper and lower factions after a long and fierce civil war between followers of the ancient Egyptian gods Horus and Seth. As a result, the country was united and symbols of both gods were marked on his crown. During his reign, he built several glorious temples and monuments in Egypt including a huge fortress in Nekhen and a large tomb at the necropolis of the sacred city of Abydos, where he was buried. Pharaoh Khasekhemwy's contribution to the project success lies in the huge assets, resources, and political stability he brought about to the country during his reign, which later enabled the establishment of the Old Kingdom and construction of the Djoser Step Pyramid.

Pharaoh Djoser, who reigned from 2670 to 2650 BCE, is the son of pharaoh Khasekhemwy and the first pharaoh of ancient Egypt's Third Dynasty, the dynasty that marks the beginning of the Old Kingdom. During Pharaoh Djoser's reign, the country witnessed a remarkable renaissance. Pharaoh Djoser's early decision upon accession to the throne was to move ancient Egypt's political capital from Thinis in Upper Egypt to Memphis in Lower Egypt. That was followed by launching a major Pharaohdom-wide construction and modernization campaign. Out of all Pharaoh Djoser's accomplishments, the Step Pyramid at Saqqara Necropolis stands out proud and tall. It was built to reflect strength and glory of his character and era. Moreover, in 2650 BCE, Pharaoh Djoser was buried in a deep burial chamber underneath the step pyramid.

Imhotep, who lived in the 27th-century BCE in ancient Egypt, is the vizier of Pharaoh Djoser and a polymath. He began his life in the temple of Memphis where he learned several crafts and skills, and where he later became the highest priest of Ptah, the demiurge of Memphis. Imhotep was also a chief architect, chief chemist, master stone maker, mathematician, and astrologist. He delivered numerous infrastructure and temple construction projects all over Upper and Lower Egypt. His legacy and masterpiece however remains the Step Pyramid complex. Imhotep outlived Pharaoh Djoser by a few years, then died and buried in Saqqara necropolis. The exact location of his tomb is however still unknown to date. In a rare historical occurrence, Imhotep got deified after his death for his skills in medicine. Imhotep's temples in Memphis were often crowded with sufferers who prayed and slept there with the conviction that the god would reveal remedies to them in their dream [1].

2.1 Exposition: Pharaoh Djoser's Accession to the Throne

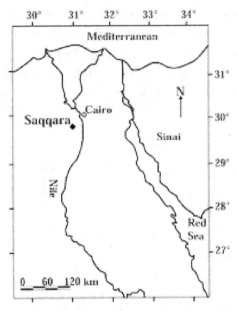

Figure 2.2 Map of ancient Egypt showing location of Saqqara necropolis [5]

It's Egypt, in the year 2670 BCE, a great year in Egypt's history. And, it's the Nile River, a great river running through Egypt's dusty deserts, as shown in Figure 2.2. The country is in celebration of the new king and the folks are cheering. The great Pharaoh Djoser, son of the great Pharaoh Khasekhemwy, accesses the throne to establish and become the first pharaoh of the Third Dynasty. The young and energetic Pharaoh Djoser was full of life and ambition. The folks got excited and you can hear sounds of festivity and celebration all over the country. The political scene at the time of Pharaoh Khasekhemwy was very turbulent. Years full of wars and fierce fights over sovereignty and dominance of Egypt's Upper and Lower Egypt's territories. When the dust of the wars had settled,

Pharaoh Khasekhemwy emerged happy and victorious. He conquered his enemies and unified Upper and Lower Egypt territories and forces. The nation was ready for a major renaissance and upturn. All the elements required to launch a major renaissance became available, including high moral spirits, political stability, tremendous assets, and vast resources. The young Pharaoh Djoser realized the opportunity made available to him, to make history, change the face of the nation, and leave behind greatness that's hard to surpass. The main task for the new Pharaoh was to rally people behind him, and most importantly, to choose the right assistants. He chose Imhotep to be his vizier and catalyst for renaissance and greatness. Figure 2.3 shows Pharaoh Djoser rushing to a popular celebration, perfectly portraying the young new Pharaoh's happy and passionate character and spirits.

Figure 2.3 Pharaoh Djoser rushing to a popular celebration [6]

Pharaoh Djoser was swift in putting his ambitions into action and his men to work. He sent expeditions to Sinai to mine for turquoise and copper, skilled farmers to boost farming and agriculture along the Nile River, and top builders to put up numerous temples and shrines across the country. And, as the diamond of the crown, Pharaoh Djoser ordered the construction of his own royal tomb. The royal tomb had to be glorious, ground-breaking, and visibly unsurpassed. The basic requirements for royal tombs at the time were to merely resist wild animals, grave robbers, and Nile floods. The requirements and expectations for the young pharaoh's royal tomb were way beyond that. The vision was to have a masterpiece that reflects the great renaissance lying ahead. The budget is open and the time frame is to match the pharaoh's expected life span. The design philosophy was to grant the pharaoh a sure and safe pathway to heaven.

2.2 Rising Action: Imhotep Proceeds With the Step Pyramid's Design and Construction

Immediately, Imhotep got to work starting with the selection of the royal tomb construction site. At this point, he did not have full imagination of how the royal tomb will ultimately look like. However, the master builder realized the fundamental importance of selecting proper site location before proceeding with design and construction. Site location was the first and most important decision that helped the pyramid survive for thousands of years. On the west side of the Nile River, right below the Nile Delta, laid a great rock plateau. The rock plateau served as a suitable solid bedrock for founding heavy pyramid. That's the Saqqara necropolis area located north west of the Ancient Egyptian capital Memphis. Saqqara necropolis was the royal graveyard for pharaohs and nobles. So the new royal tomb location would be somewhere within Saqqara, however applying the basics. A royal tomb must be located and designed to satisfy three main criteria, namely, massive and remarkable, safe against wild animals and robbers, and most importantly safe against eradication by Nile River floods. Imhotep selected a strategic limestone platform in Saqqara Necropolis overseeing the majestic graveyard. The platform was ca 40 m higher than the water level in the adjacent Nile River and outside of the Nile valley where the yearly flooding takes place. Such high level is also required to accommodate the deep shafts leading to the Pharaoh's burial chamber, which must stay in the dry region above the highest ground water table. The selected strategic tomb location safeguarded the eternal structure from floods or getting buried in the desert sands.

Pharaoh Djoser's instruction was with immediate effect, therefore, Imhotep, under time pressure, had to start the construction on site straightaway. In order to do that, he needed a tomb design, construction material, and workers both skilled and unskilled. The norm in tomb design of ancient Egyptian royal tombs at this point in time was the mud-brick "mastaba," or the "pr-djt," meaning house of eternity in Ancient Egyptian. A mastaba is a solid flat-roofed rectangular superstructure with inward sloping sides made of sun-dried Nile River mudbricks. As shown in Figure 2.4, typical mastaba design would consist of the mentioned bulk of mudbricks, a small chapel with statue, and a deep shaft (or two, one real and one false) leading to the burial chamber. Mastabas were built in various sizes, usually of 9-m height and the rectangular longer side about two to four times the shorter side. Mastabas were also always oriented in the North–South direction, which was believed to be essential for the deceased's access to the afterlife.

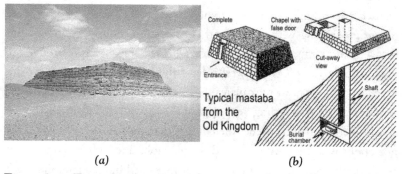

(a)   (b)

Figure 2.4 Example of ancient egyptian mastaba design and construction (a) Photo of Mastaba [7] and (b) Sketch of Mastaba [8]

The departure from the norm, that is the mastaba tombs, required talent, resources, and authority, which were all available to Imhotep. So despite the time pressure and urge to start construction immediately, he took several change decisions. As to tomb design, he changed the mastaba shape from a rectangular pointing North to a North–South–East–West (NSEW) square. A seemingly minor change; however, a major departure from the norm which will prevail in later dynasties. The start-up mastaba had modest dimensions of 63 m × 63 m × 8 m. The start-up mastaba was only the start for something much bigger, and much higher.

As to construction material, Imhotep first began with traditional mudbricks, just to have a quick start, however kept thinking. The pharaoh's expectations were much higher than just another mudbrick mastaba. He kept sharpening his thoughts until the idea of switching to cut limestone came to his mind, along with a big smile and sparkling eyes. Although today such a change seems simple, at the time it was a major paradigm shift. The smile suddenly disappeared when he remembered that cutting stones is a tough job requiring a lot of skilled resources. However, that was not an issue, for the project was royal, and Imhotep was the pharaoh's vizier. The decision to switch to stone was clearly affected by two factors, namely, Imhotep's background as a stone maker, and stories of mudbrick tomb collapses in earlier dynasties. The innovative use of solid stone bricks changed the rules of the construction game at large. It opened the way for the construction of bigger and higher buildings, in this project, as well as in later stone dynasties. The reason is that limestone has a much higher compressive strength than the mudbricks, which dominated construction until this point. As to sourcing of the limestone blocks, Imhotep decided to mine immediately around the site. An early sustainable construction mentality. After mining was done, a 750-m long by 40-m wide trench was already formed all around the construction site forming what's called the "great trench." The great trench will later serve as a security feature to safeguard the step pyramid complex against invaders.

Construction workers were made available in masses for the royal task. Cutting stones, moving cut-stone blocks to the tomb location, and laying stones horizontally in layers in the same way they used to lay mudbricks. Workers were happy and inspired to participate in the prestigious construction of the demigod Pharaoh's royal tomb. For the highly religious culture and society of believers, that was a sacred assignment. As such, workers came to the site motivated and ready to work hard happily. So the men immediately got to work, and Imhotep entered his creative mode. As time went by, his creative mind continued to ponder and contemplate, then sparked with the big decision. That is, to go higher with the tomb. The final size and height of the tomb were still not decided; however, the decision to go bigger and higher was established in Imhotep's mind. As is common in going beyond the state of the art and achieving breakthroughs, the design and construction progressed incrementally. The step pyramid zigzagged its way to completion horizontally and vertically in a well-orchestrated manner. The incremental design information included both the superstructure of the pyramid as well as the underground substructure including a maze of deep shafts, galleries, and burial chambers. The pyramid construction progressed in stages, first the initial at-grade mastaba, then one higher and smaller mastaba atop of the other, until a four-tier step pyramid is shaped. At this stage, Imhotep invited Pharaoh Djoser to visit the site and see the innovative tomb. The pharaoh liked the idea, but however thought the pyramid should go even higher. Imhotep got the message and got back to work to make history. As shown in Figure 2.5, he enlarged the pyramid's basis and added two more tiers to reach 6 tiers and 62.5-m height to become the highest building in the world at the time. In the last stage, he finally cladded the step pyramid with polished limestone.

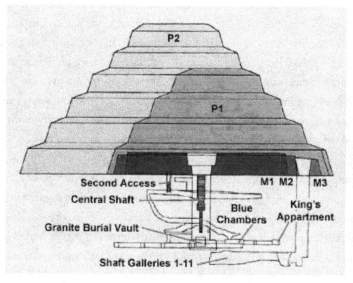

Figure 2.5 Step-Pyramid evolution of design and construction stages [9]

The following step-by-step construction procedure describes the Step Pyramid's design and construction stages and provides a discussion of the background and objectives of each design and construction stage. It also describes how design overlapped with construction and how design information was disseminated incrementally, to keep the construction going while satisfying tomb design and functional requirements.

M1 Mastaba—The Initial Platform

Stage M1 is the initial start-up mastaba. Started early in a rush upon Pharaoh Djoser's instruction to proceed. Oriented NSEW believed to lead to eternity. Introduced two pivotal mastaba construction innovations, namely, made of ca 30-cm cut-stone instead of mudbricks, and, took a square shape instead of the rectangular shape that prevailed in earlier dynasties. Measured 63 m × 63 m × 8 m height.

M2 Mastaba—Extension on All Four Sides

Stage M2 included the expansion of mastaba M1 on all four sides using slightly bigger ca 38-cm cut-stone blocks to reach 71.5 m × 71.5 m. The extension however was 1-m lower than M1, that is 7 m instead of 8-m high. This drop in mastaba height has a significant engineering function. It forms a horizontal tooth or shear key that's needed to prevent a plane sliding surface between M2 and the upcoming higher stone layers.

M3 Mastaba—Extension Eastward and Underground Maze

Stage M3 included further mastaba expansion on the east side only by 8 m so new size reached 79.5 m × 71.5 m. The extension however was 2-m lower than M2, that is 5 m instead of 7-m high. This drop in M3 height along with the drop in M2 height formed a sawtooth effect, preventing horizontal shear slippage at the interface with the upcoming higher stone layers, especially in the wake of eccentric construction and when subjected to major wind and earthquake external lateral loads. The 8-m expansion served as a working platform for the construction of 11 deep shafts of variable depths reaching 33 m, leading to a common gallery at about 20-m depth. The northern shafts were later used for the burial of royal family. This stage also included the construction of a major 7-m wide central shaft, the pharaoh's burial chamber, in addition to ca 5.5 km of tunnels and galleries of various sizes.

P1 Pyramid—The Bulk of the Step Pyramid—First Enlargement

Stage P1 involved the step pyramid construction proceeding upward and gradually shrinking inward as the pyramid goes higher, thus forming a step pyramid shape. At the P1 stage the pyramid reached 85.5-m long × 77-m wide and 42-m high, made of 4 tiers inclined at 84 degrees. It was built using ca 52-cm thick cut-stones. The source of stones was the great trench dug around the site, which played a dual role, a sustainable source for limestone blocks, and later on as an artificial obstacle to safeguard the funeral complex. The construction limestone blocks were designed to resemble the form and size of large mudbricks. A genius engineering method was used by laying stone blocks not simply vertically but in courses inclined toward the center of the pyramid. That significantly increased its structural stability and would be the secret why the step pyramid lasted stable and standing-still for thousands of years.

P2 Pyramid—The Bulk of the Pyramid—Final Enlargement and Stone Cladding

Stage P2 increased the step pyramid size substantially to reach 121-m length × 107-m width and 62.5-m height, made of 6 tiers inclined at 84 degrees. It was also built using the ca 52-cm-thick cut-stones. The massive step pyramid body was then covered by a layer of fair polished limestone cladding, and the gap between cladding and the rough pyramid stone body was filled with packing material.

The design and construction of the Step Pyramid took about 19 years' time. The rate of construction progress fluctuated through the course of the years pending resources availability. In summer, during the Nile River flooding periods, progress accelerated. Farmers were idle, so came to give hand in cutting, digging deep shafts, or cutting stones in the great trench. The Step Pyramid construction was completed successfully attracting major attention from all over Egypt and neighboring civilizations.

2.3 Climax: Project Completion and Celebration

When completed in 2650 BCE, Pharaoh Djoser's Step Pyramid was the highest building in the world. A major construction by far exceeding any other construction at the time and taking a shape that is never seen or even imagined before. An awe-inspiring spectacular high and white monument and royal tomb symbolizing a stairway to heaven. The Step Pyramid itself was only the crown diamond of a vast complex including several structures serving both life and afterlife functions. Those included a collection of temples, chapels, pavilions, corridors, storerooms, and halls. The 15-ha complex was built on a north–south axis and surrounded by a wall of limestone 10.5-m high of a design resembling mudbrick works. For security purposes, the wall design included 14 doors, 13 of which were false and only one was a real entrance. For further security and to make the complex hard to access for unwanted strangers, the entire complex was surrounded by a 750-m long and 40-m wide trench. Figure 2.6 shows a rendering of the Pharaoh Djoser's Step Pyramid Complex as it looked like at the time it was built and inaugurated.

On the day of inauguration, the elegant white step pyramid was shining in the sun rays, catching the sights in an awe-inspiring scene. The sunshiny step pyramid was so spectacular that it even attracted the attention of the sun god "Ra." A great sign of gods' satisfaction and thus a pharaoh's happy eternal afterlife. Pharaoh Djoser, his retinue, the entire nation, and the whole universe, moved to Saqqara Necropolis to witness the inauguration of the innovative royal tomb step pyramid. He looked up at the shining step pyramid with a big smile, sighed deeply, shined on, and then passed away. Pharaoh Djoser's body was mummified and moved carefully to the deep burial room, in a major burial ceremony, witnessed by all creatures of the universe.

At the end of the inauguration day, the sun set, marking the end of a greatly joyful, and deeply sad day. Everyone went back to their earthly life, and the glorious pharaoh went on to eternal life through his royal step pyramid.

Night took over, and darkness and silence prevailed.

Figure 2.6 Pharaoh Djoser step pyramid complex—rendering [10]

2.4 Falling Action: Aging Over the Thousands of Years

Pharaoh Djoser died in 2650 BCE, followed by Imhotep in 2600 BCE, leaving behind a great eternal legacy. However, and as at all times, when creators of greatness die, their achievements suffer abandonment, and even worse than that. The king is dead, long live the king! A bitter fact of life. Therefore, after the departure of Pharaoh Djoser and Imhotep, the great Step Pyramid and its mortal complex were abandoned for thousands of years. "Unfortunately, all of the precautions and intricate design of the underground complex did not prevent ancient robbers from finding a way in. Djoser's grave goods, and even his mummy, were stolen at some point in the past and all archaeologists found of the king was parts of his mummified foot and a few valuables overlooked by the thieves. There was enough left to examine throughout the pyramid and its complex, however, to amaze the archaeologists who excavated it" [11]. In addition, time and lack of care and maintenance took their toll on the step pyramid's stone cladding, which almost disappeared, as shown in Figure 2.7. In fact, the whole development almost disappeared and buried in the sands of Saqqara desert until recently during Napoleon Bonaparte's campaign on Egypt in 1798 to 1801 AD. Napoleon brought a team of scientists and researchers who did a great job in exploring the abandoned monuments of ancient Egypt. The work of Napoleon's team was instrumental in opening up the Ancient Egyptian civilization to the world, especially with the deciphering of the Egyptian hieroglyphs. That opened up a wide door to reading the true stories painted or carved on walls of the temples and monuments. The following figure illustrates a recent aerial photograph of Pharaoh Djoser's Step Pyramid Complex.

Figure 2.7 Pharaoh Djoser step pyramid complex—recent aerial photograph [11]

The true discovery and salvation of the Pharaoh Djoser's Step Pyramid and Complex occurred a century later in the 1920 AD with the involvement of the English archaeologist Cecil Mallaby Firth (1878–1931 AD), then the French architect and Archeologist Jean-Philippe Lauer (1902–2001 AD), who spent 75 years of his life busy with the discovery and restoration of Pharaoh Djoser's Step Pyramid and its mortuary complex. In 1992 AD, a major earthquake hit the region and shook the step pyramid and its complex to the point of near collapse. The earthquake left gaps and cavities in the step pyramid's body and affected its underlying maze of tunnels. International and local efforts were put into the case trying to preserve and restore the major world monument. These efforts have been limited success and the fact of the matter would appear to be that the earthquake has indeed weakened the great step pyramid to some extent.

The construction of Pharaoh Djoser's Step Pyramid marked the beginning of an era of pyramids. It became the preferred architectural model for Ancient Egyptian spiritual philosophy and principles. Later in the Third Dynasty, at least two other major royal pyramids were attempted, however left unfinished owing to the short reigns of their related pharaohs. The real age of pyramids was the Fourth Dynasty, the time when most of the well-known pyramids were built, including the Great Pyramids of Giza/Egypt. In a rare occurrence, Imhotep got worshiped long after his death for his legacy in the field of medicine and healing. In the Greco-Roman times, Imhotep's temples in Memphis were crowded with patients from Europe who came seeking therapies and remedies.

2.5 Resolution: Pharaoh Djoser's Step Pyramid Today

Today, Pharaoh Djoser's Step Pyramid at its complex forms a key site of UNESCO's list of world heritage. The unique ancient monument has added a great legacy to the human history and the history of architecture and construction. It currently attracts over millions of tourists to Saqqara Memphis Egypt every year. Today, in the 21st century, more than 47 centuries after his departure, Imhotep is still a world renowned figure, hailed by many groups to be the father of Architecture of all times. The Step Pyramid and its complex are considered to be the first documented Design–Build construction project in the world, preceding the Great Pyramids of Giza Egypt. They left a great legacy and inspiring story of innovation and passion in construction and determination to bring about construction greatness. Secrets and wonders of the step pyramid complex are still being uncovered by modern archeologists and architect. A due attribution goes to the great French Architect, Archaeologist, and Egyptologist Jean-Philippe Lauer, 1902 to 2001 AD, who dedicated 75 years of his life in Saqqara Memphis Egypt revealing the secrets and restoring the treasures of the Pharaoh Djoser's Step Pyramid and its cryptic complex.

Story Recap Illustrated on Story Plot Diagram

The following Figure 2.8 provides overview and recap of the story spread along the five components of the typical story telling plot diagram, namely, Exposition, Rising Action, Climax, Falling Action, and Resolution.

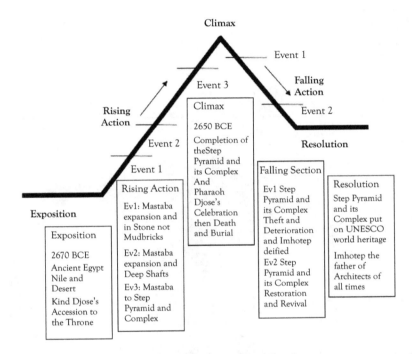

Figure 2.8 The Step Pyramid story on story plot diagram

CHAPTER 3

The Empire State Building, New York, USA— John Raskob and the Amazing NYC Race into the Sky

It's 1929 AD in New York City, New York, USA.

While plans for the construction of the Empire State Building were being finalized, a fierce competition erupted over the title of the "World's Tallest Building." Chrysler Building was about to win the "Race into the Sky" when the Empire State Building gets into play determined to make a spectacular win, and the story begins.

Figure 3.1 The Empire State Building—New York, USA [1]

Table of Contents

Preface

Greatness in construction can be defined by a great design, great impact on the economy, or even a great construction process or technology. The Empire State Building, shown in Figure 3.1, embodied all these qualities and added to them great leadership and great timing. The Great Depression hitting the United States, Wall Street, and New York City after a decade of prosperity and growth. The economy is in a state of shock and awe and many businesses were shrinking or just coming to a standstill. That's when great minds get to work turning the crisis to opportunity. After all, material prices are down and resources are overflowing. That's when the New Yorkers decided to build the tallest building in the world in a heated race to the sky. The Empire State, Inc. decided to join the race with an office building in Midtown Manhattan, and appointed John Raskob to take the lead on project delivery. The directive was to build the highest building possible, as fast as possible. John Raskob began with securing the project's political support and funding scheme, then appointing the right design and construction team. The motivated team turned the site into a vibrating workshop, and the outcome will be the tallest building in the world completed in a record time.

What Makes This Project Great

The Empire State Building marks the start of the tall buildings construction mania that spread all over the world in the 20th century to date. Moreover, the following 10 points explain why the Empire State Building is great by any measure or standard:

1. The tallest building in the world at the time it was completed.
2. Ironically the tallest building in NYC "twice," first in 1931 AD then again in September 2001 AD.
3. The first building in history to exceed the 100 floors line being itself 102 floors high.
4. Built at the beginning of the Great Depression in the United States defying economic feasibility.
5. The world's fastest tower construction of an incredible pace of ca 1-m height per day.
6. One of The Seven Wonders of the Modern World as determined by the American Society of Civil Engineers in 1994 AD.
7. A major tourist destination visited yearly by 4 million tourists from around the world.
8. Listed in the U.S. National Register of Historic Places as a National Historic Landmark.
9. Perfectly symbolizes the Art Deco building style that prevailed after the First World War.
10. Imposed its unique architectural style of tall buildings around the world.

Story Starring and Key Characters

This story is starred by all project participants, in particular the great unknown laborers and their families; without their contribution, greatness would not have been achieved.

Table 3.1 Story starring and key characters

John Raskob [2]	Name	John Jacob Raskob
	Party	The Empire State Inc.
	Title	Democratic National Committee Chair 1928–1932 AD
	Legacy	An American entrepreneur and businessman. Led the major companies DuPont and General Motors before leading the funding, vision, and realization of the Empire State Building.
	PM Role	Project Sponsor, Investor, Owner
William Lamb [3]	Name	William Frederick Lamb
	Party	Designer, Shreve, Lamb, and Harmon Associates
	Title	Designer of the Empire State Building
	Legacy	Designed numerous notable projects in NYC including Forbes Magazine, Standard Oil, and General Motors buildings. Awarded an honorary doctorate from Williams College in 1932 AD.
	PM Role	Project Manager, Design
William Starrett [4]	Name	William Aiken Starrett
	Party	Contractor, "Starrett Brothers and Eken, Inc."
	Title	Builder of the Empire State Building
	Legacy	Built numerous skyscrapers in NYC and the USA. President of the Starrett Brothers, Inc. Awarded an honorary doctorate from Michigan University in 1931 AD. Nicknamed the father of skyscrapers.
	PM Role	Project Manager, Construction

John Jacob Raskob, 1879–1950 AD, is an American financial executive and businessman. He led DuPont and General Motors before leading the vision, funding, and realization of the Empire State Building. John Raskob, served as Chairman of the Democratic National Committee between 1928 and 1932 AD and led the 1928 AD U.S. presidential campaign for Alfred Emanuel Smith. John Raskob was a keen investor in the NYSE stock market in the 1920s AD; however, luckily, he ceased speculation almost a year before the stock market crashed in October 1929 AD. During the decade of the Great Depression, which followed the NYSE crash, John Raskob focused on the investment in the Empire State Building. The building won the NYC race into the sky competition and became the world's tallest building. John Raskob passed away in 1950 AD at the age of 71 leaving behind the world's iconic Empire State Building as his main career legacy.

William Frederick Lamb, 1883–1952 AD, is an American architect and Art Deco designer of many landmark buildings in New York City and the United States. William Lamb is best known as the chief designer of the iconic Empire State Building in NYC. He graduated from Williams College in 1904 AD and then obtained a diploma at the École des Beaux-Arts in Paris France in 1911 AD. William Lamb joined the New York-based architectural firm Carrère & Hastings where he became a partner in 1920 AD, and the firm was later renamed to "Shreve, Lamb and Harmon" in 1929 AD. After his spectacular design of the Empire State Building, William Lamb received an honorary doctorate from Williams College in 1932 AD. Lamb was a member of the American Academy of Arts and Letters, the Art Commission of the City of New York, and the Architectural League of New York.

William Aiken Starrett, 1877–1932 AD, is an American architect and a pioneer builder of skyscrapers, so nicknamed as the "father of the skyscrapers." William Starrett is best known as the builder of the

Empire State Building in NYC. He began his construction career in 1895 AD at the age of 18 joining companies that build skyscrapers. Over the years, he gained specialized experience in the design and construction of high-rise buildings that can resist earthquakes. In 1901 AD, he joined his brothers in the contracting and real estate business. In 1922 AD, he became president of the Starrett Corporation. He delivered over 200 buildings and skyscrapers all over the United States. After his construction of the Empire State Building, William Starrett obtained an honorary Doctor of Engineering in 1931 AD. Starrett was a member of the American Society of Civil Engineers, American Society of Mechanical Engineers, and the Associated General Contractors of America.

3.1 Exposition: Great Ambition Defying Great Depression

It's NYC in the 1920 AD, with sights and ambience as shown in Figure 3.2. The elegant life is starting to move gradually toward Upper Manhattan, leaving behind the once classy Waldorf-Astoria hotel, just an outdated building set for sale. In 1928 AD, the hotel got closed and sold to Bethlehem Engineering Corporation. Acting traditionally, the corporation planned to pull down the old hotel and come up with a mere 25-story office building. Bethlehem's plan lacking energy just failed fast and the hotel got resold. The new buyer is The Empire State Inc., a young and powerful company owned by a group of wealthy investors, cleverly named after New York, the Empire State. The ambitious young company strengthens its proposition by appointing a powerful president, Alfred Emanuel Smith, the four-time former Governor of New York and the U.S. Democratic Party's 1928 AD presidential candidate. Having in mind to bring about a construction greatness, and driven by a sky-high ambition, the company buys the adjacent land so having a substantial combined plot measuring 130-m wide by 61-m long, enough to build something big that can change the world.

Figure 3.2 Aerial view of Lower Manhattan—construction boom in 1924 AD [5]

It's NYC in the year 1928 AD. The nation is living a great decade of economic boom and construction growth. The world is witnessing a growing popularity of the Art Deco style. NYC is busy building modern Art Deco and is growing fast. Wall Street numbers are mouthwatering for investors. The real estate development is at an unprecedented peak. Construction of skyscrapers is becoming a trend fueled by a heated desire to build high, a contest that was nicknamed by the popular media as "Race into the Sky." The overarching goal in the construction industry is to maintain the NYC status as home of the tallest building in the world. The world's tallest building at the time was the Woolworth Building in NYC built in 1913 AD with a mere height of 241 m.

Meanwhile in NYC, an Art Deco skyscrapers ambitious race into the sky was going on mainly between Bank of Manhattan Building and Chrysler Building. The Empire State Inc. decided to join the race and started looking for a suitable piece of land to build the underdog skyscraper in place of Waldorf-Astoria hotel. In October 1929 AD, the demolition of the doomed hotel began. Fueled by the passion and rush to build the Empire State Building, the demolition process of the old and sturdy building took place in a superfast pace. Much of the wreckage and rubble that made up the old hotel, including granite and bronze, was merely dumped into the ocean somewhere near New Jersey. Chrysler Building was grooming to become the world's tallest building. However, "The Race into the Sky" was far from over, as the near future will show. The story began with the Great Depression hitting NYC and the world. On Tuesday October 29, 1929 AD, following period of speculation, NYSE traded over 16 million shares in a single day, causing a tragic stock market crash. Many billions of dollars were lost, wiping out thousands of businesses. That day was called Black Tuesday.

The stock market crash took its toll on the construction market and real estate development. Many projects got canceled or shelved leaving the Empire State Inc. in a go/no-go limbo as to whether or not to proceed with their ambitious office building. It was a defining moment in the struggle between the great ambition and the Great Depression. And guess what, great ambition won as John Raskob decided to go ahead with the project, no matter what. That's despite the market crash and the steep decrease in the demand for office buildings. Luckily, unlike most real estate developers NYC, John Raskob happened to have stopped speculating months before the stock market crash. That gave him a favorable credit status that enabled him to get the funding required to build the project. So, while Waldorf-Astoria hotel was being demolished, Raskob was arranging project funding and finances. While doing that, Raskob the clever entrepreneur argued that the economic crisis is indeed an opportunity taking advantage of the reduced construction material cost and the vast construction resources and material suppliers made available, thanks to the stoppage of many construction projects in NYC and across the country.

3.2 Rising Action: The Race Into the Sky Goes Well Underway

In November 2019 AD, the Empire State Inc. awarded the Empire State Building's design to the famous and experienced architecture firm Shreve, Lamb, and Harmon Associates. The vision of John Raskob communicated to the team was to build the highest skyscraper possible, in the shortest time possible, and the building has got to be the tallest in the world. John Raskob took a jumbo pencil, stood it on its end, and looked at the architect William Lamb saying: "Bill, how high can you make the building so that it won't fall down?" Time was of essence, so the talented architect William

Lamb got direct into action, producing the first building drawings in just two weeks. He chose a compelling Art Deco architectural style that looked like a sturdy pencil pointing to the sky. In doing that, the architect William Lamb was affected by earlier high-rise building designs, namely, the Reynolds Building in Winston-Salem/North Carolina, shown in Figure 3.3. The Empire State Building's elegant sturdy Art-Deco high-rise design style will later on, in its turn, inspire numerous architects from all over the world and will win numerous architectural awards.

Figure 3.3 Reynolds Building in Winston-Salem, North Carolina, USA [6]

As usual in creative design, the building design process went through 15 iterations and cycles of development and refinement until perfected. The first conceptual sketches produced by architect William Lamb only showed a 50-story high building, that is, one story higher than the 49-story high Carew Tower, a tower that inspired Lamb. Lamb's ambitions were however much higher, and so certainly were ambitions of Raskob and the Empire State Inc. The competition and race to the sky go on, mainly with the key rival the Chrysler Building. The Empire State Inc.'s team was monitoring the Chrysler Building's height, which was increasing gradually. The Empire State Building's height has therefore also started to increase gradually from 50 to 60 stories and then to a daring 80-story height to reach 1,050 ft height and thus to exceed the Chrysler Building's height of 1,046 ft. That necessitated a wider building base and larger foot print. That was quick and fast secured by the Empire State Inc.'s Alfred Smith who acquired additional land of the adjacent lot 27–31 West 33rd Street, thus adding 23 m (75 ft) strip width to the building's site. Figure 3.4 shows the building's concept design stage isometric sketch produced by the project architect. Sketch shows the building shape, masses, set-backs, heights, and status of compliance with the building code.

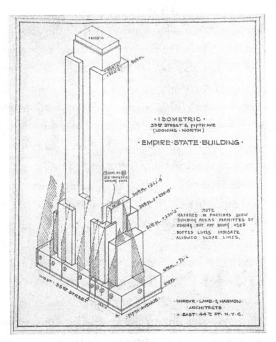

Figure 3.4 Shreve, Lamb, and Harmon's initial sketch of the Empire State Building [7]

At this point, the architectural design seemed to be finished and building size and shape agreed, so time to proceed to construction. This is when John Raskob got into the picture again flagging up a key point and bringing about another major project decision. A decision that is only second to his first decision to go ahead with the project in the first place despite the stock market crash. The clever Raskob noticed that the Empire State Building's height of 320 m (1,050 ft) would only be 1.2 m (4 ft) higher than the rival Chrysler Building. Such a risky marginal difference could eventually be sorted by Chrysler in a last minute rod extension, resulting in a catastrophic loss of the world's tallest tower status. The observation was acknowledged by the team and William Lamb had a clever response to it. He checked the building design and came back with the great news that the building can indeed be extended by further 16 additional stories, that is 61 m or 200 ft, thus finishing the race to the sky once and for all. The proposed change was approved by Raskob and the mood changed from fear and suspicion to enthusiasm and passion. The Empire State Building tower will be the king of all towers, so deserved a crown. A remarkable Art Deco metal crown was added to the building head. That also availed further building height. The final building height would then sum up to 443.2 m (1,454 ft). The Chrysler Building finished second with just 319 m (1,046 ft) height. History doesn't remember those who come in second positions. In appreciation of the upcoming world's tallest building, the NYC Municipal Authorities placed a 30-story height restriction on the nearby buildings surrounding the Empire State Building. That gave the building open city views from all directions and made it seen clearly from quite a long distance. Figure 3.5 shows the final design dimensions of the Empire State Building, good for construction.

In December 1929 AD, the Empire State Inc. secured a $27.5 million loan from the Metropolitan Life Insurance Company. That action gave the start signal to the skyscraper engineering and construction teams to begin and proceed at the maximum safe speed. The construction contract was awarded to the renowned American contractor "Starrett Brothers and Eken." Construction was entrusted to the skyscrapers guru William Aiken Starrett. Project was scheduled to complete by May 1, 1931 AD, setting a challenging task on both the design and the construction teams, especially that design of the skyscraper was yet to be completed. This turned the project into a perfect form of the design–build project delivery approach, in which design and construction activities proceed in parallel using Concurrent Engineering. The strong project leadership by John

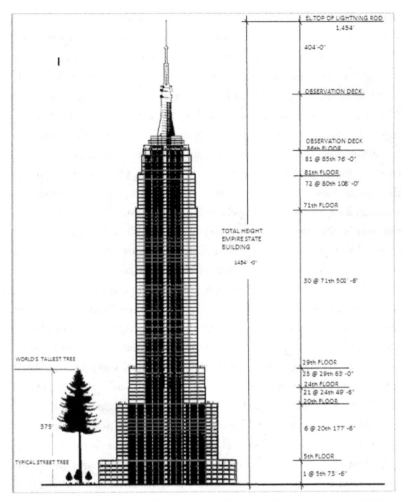

Figure 3.5 Empire State Building final design dimensions (available in word format)

Raskob and the competence and maturity of the designer and contractor enabled the parties to synchronize working together as one integrated team, and hence actuate the power of the design–build approach.

On January 12, 1930 AD, a structural steel contract was awarded to the "American Bridge" as a structural steel manufacturer supported mainly by Bethlehem Steel for colossal steel members. Steel members were fabricated at Ambridge, Pittsburgh/Pennsylvania plant, ca 370 miles away from the jobsite in NYC. That necessitated the application of the "just-in-time" strategy for the delivery and supply of steel members to the construction site. On January 22, site excavation started even before completing the demolition of the Waldorf-Astoria hotel. Racing with time, two 12-hour work shifts, 300 men each, worked continuously to dig into, to rock the 17 m (55 ft) excavation pit and reinforced concrete piles. On March 17, 1930 AD excavation was nearly completed and construction of the building structural works started. This date marked the official start of construction.

While placing the first steel columns on the completed reinforced concrete footings, other footings were being built. On April 1, 1930 AD, the steel framework members started to arrive at the site continuously in a seamless supply, electrifying the site and the team. Since project location was in city streets, work had to use a just-in-time strategy, that is, no material storage on site. For instance, steel structure elements were fabricated in Pittsburg, 370 miles away, then shipped to the jobsite to arrive "just-in-time" and be picked up right away by site cranes and brought to the location where they are to be erected and bolted together. Moreover, the team developed an innovative linear construction execution plan, as shown in Figure 3.6. The linear schedule was used to plan and control progress of the design and construction of the steel skeleton in a logical repetitive work sequence applicable to each floor of the building. The repetitive work cycle included five consecutive steps, namely, (1) Requesting Information and general layout design drawings indicating sizes and quantities of the required steel elements; (2) placing mill orders to produce the required steel sections; (3) obtaining the design and fabrication details required to fabricate the required steel members; (4) delivery of the prefabricated steel members from Ambridge steel fabrication plant in Pittsburg to the jobsite; and, finally (5) erection of the steel members and moving up with the building.

The combination of just-in-time delivery and linear scheduling enabled high levels of efficiency, and resulted in the Empire State Building being finished in a record time that will be hard to beat for generations to come. The impact of the powerful combination can be traced everywhere in the project, in particular in the A–Z flow of design information feeding into manufacturing through to transportation and site installation. The project was largely design–build, so in many cases the upstream design information required to initiate a downstream manufacturing, transportation,

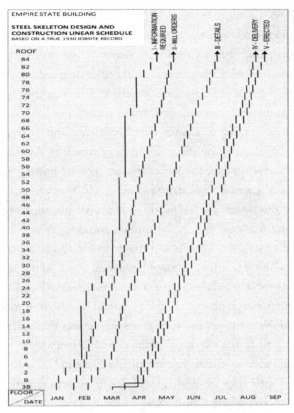

Figure 3.6 Linear scheduling of steel skeleton design and construction in 1930 AD [8]

and construction activities had to be released just-in-time to meet the microscopic scheduled dates for site installation. Another example is the Indiana limestone façade cladding, which had to be ordered, engineered, cut to size, shipped to site, and erected in place, all just-in-time. Likewise, finishes, doors, windows, building services, elevators, decorations all had to be finalized and moved on from a process step to the next until final installation in just-in-time environment. In fact, due to the project's extremely tight schedule, it could be comfortably stated that most of the project activities whether design, procurement, or construction had to be carried out in just-in-time tact and pace, and the result was simply making history.

"Sky Boys" is another story of greatness and glory of the Empire State Building. Greatness in construction was most reflected in the over 3,400 construction workers who participated in the construction of the legendary skyscraper. Construction workers showed extraordinary skill and bravery, especially in "working at height." The way they looked and operated was just phenomenal. You would see them walking on sky-high steel beams or hanging to a cable with confidence and in ways that are creative and at times quite scary. Technology wise, the sky boys utilized a system of well-engineered railway cars and material-hosting equipment to pick up and transport construction materials from the ground up to and around the skyscraper. Transported materials included over 55,000 tons of structural steel and ca 10 million building façade bricks, and much more construction goods and materials for all construction disciplines. As to be expected, construction workers attracted the attention of the popular media, which nicknamed them as the "Sky Boys" in the first place. Media photographers took their cameras hundreds of meters high, got closer to the sky boys, and took close-up pictures that will shock and inspire the world. The sky boys' abilities and bravery were just exceptional at any scale in either modern or old history. Unfortunately, five workers lost their lives in various incidents during construction. Figure 3.7 shows a scene of the Empire State Building's sky boys taking lunch up in the air.

Figure 3.7 The Sky Boys taking lunch atop a skyscraper [9]

Figure 3.8 The Empire State Building—under construction near completion in 1931 AD [10]

By June 1930 AD, structural steel erection reached the 26th floor and proceeded to completion, as shown in Figure 3.8. By September 1930 AD, the building's steel structure topped out completing 12 days ahead of schedule. When the structural steel was completed, proud and happy the sky boys raised the U.S. flag atop the 86th floor, and the whole world applauded. That great achievement generated a huge momentum that would drive the project forward until the spectacular project completion by the end of April 1931 AD.

3.3 Climax: Project Completion and Celebration

On May 1, 1931 AD, the Empire State Building was officially completed as planned and celebrated in a major ceremonial event, as shown in Figures 3.9 and 3.10. The project achieved its hard-earned status as

Figure 3.9 The Empire State Building—roof top celebration of construction completion in 1931 AD [11]

Figure 3.10 The Empire State Building—completed construction in 1931 AD [12]

the "tallest building the world" ever built by mankind. As to the "Race to the Sky," it came first, far ahead of and higher than the underdog Chrysler Building, thus strongly winning the NYC 1928–1931 AD skyscrapers race.

The world was watching the Empire State Building opening ceremony honored by the U.S. President Herbert Hoover who turned on the building's lights with the push of a button from Washington, DC. The opening ceremony was attended by over 350 distinguished guests. On the very next day, building was officially opened to the public and advertised in local media and newspapers. Opening of the building lifted the value of properties and businesses in the proximity of the tallest building in the world located on the west side of Fifth Avenue in Manhattan, between 33rd Street to the south and 34th Street to the north. Extensive marketing efforts were exerted to promote the Empire State Building's and solidify its status as the world's tallest building. That included heavy advertising in local newspapers as well as printing observatories on local railway tickets. These efforts paid off, and the building quickly became a popular touristic attraction. Much of the building's revenue in the first year of operation came from the $1 tickets visitors had to pay to ride elevators to observation decks. The Empire State Building skyscraper factsheet includes an architectural height of 381 m (1,250 ft), tip height of 443.2 m (1,454 ft), 102 floors, 208,879 m² (2,248,355 ft²) floor area, 73 elevators, and a final development cost of $40.95 m (equivalent to $654 in 2020). Project was completed in 410 days measured from the official construction start date of March 17, 1929 AD and 464 days from the excavation start date of January 22, 1929 AD. So in a nutshell, that's roughly 444 m in 444 days.

The Empire State Building introduced a master piece of glory and charisma symbolizing the American civilization and the Art Deco style. The sturdy skyscraper stood proud and tall in the skyline of NYC attracting the attention of NYC residents and visitors and indeed the entire world. It was quick to attract industry attention and recognition. In 1931 AD, the American newspaper *Washington Star* listed it as part of one of the "seven wonders of the modern world." In 1932 AD, the skyscraper won the Fifth Avenue Association's gold medal for architectural excellence. In 1933 AD, the Hollywood global block buster movie "King

Kong" was released featuring a large ape named Kong climbing the NYC Empire State Building, thus making the building a worldwide recognizable skyscraper and a famous cinematic icon. As the tallest building in the world and the first building ever to exceed 100 floors, the Empire State Building immediately became an icon of the city, of the nation, and of the era. What spoiled the moment, however, was the aftermath of the NYSE crash occurred in October 1929 AD. The devastating effects of such crash forced many businesses to close down or shrink, and many companies had to migrate out of NYC. As a result, the demand for business offices in NYC suffered a sharp decline, leaving the new great Empire State Building almost empty.

3.4 Falling Action: Glory to Profit and Trip Through Times

The 1930s global depression took its toll on the world economy and on the economics of the Empire State Building. In the first year of operation, the building was mostly empty, prompting some New Yorker's to call it the "Empty" State Building. However, the great Empire State Building survived the crisis and came out of it strong and profitable with 90 percent of the building leased in five years. Gradually, economy got back on its feet and businesses started to get back to NYC and the building managed to break even by 1950 AD. In 1951 AD, as the economy got great again, the building developer John Raskob put the building up for sale and sold it for $51 million, which was the highest price ever paid for a single structure at the time. From this point on, the Empire State Building became so profitable and fully leased with a waiting list of businesses looking to lease space in the prestigious building. Ten years later, the Empire State Building was sold again for $61 million. In 2020 AD, the building price would certainly be expressed in terms of billions of U.S. dollars.

Apart from glory and world recognition, the Empire State Building has witnessed a weird incident that tested its structural strength and integrity. In 1945 AD, a B-25 Mitchell bomber accidentally crashed into the north side of the building between the 79th and 80th floors. One of the two aircraft engines penetrated the building landing on the roof of a nearby building, whereas the other engine and part of the landing gear fell down an elevator shaft causing fire. The sturdy building took the blow with coolness and persistence and was reopened partially on many floors a couple of days later after the incident.

In 1970 AD, the Empire State lost its position as the world's tallest office building to the in NYC World Trade Center Twin-Towers. Ironically, the Empire State Building reclaimed its NYC title in 2001 following the destruction of the World Trade Center 415.1 m (1,362 ft) during September 11 attacks, however, before losing it again in 2013 AD to the One World Trade Center tower 546.2 m (1,792 ft) located at Ground Zero next to the footprint of World Trade Center Twin-Towers in NYC.

3.5 Resolution: The Empire State Building Today

Today, the Empire State Building is more than just a tall building or even an icon of New York City or the United States. It's a symbol of pride and inspiration for the entire construction community all over the world. Although not the world's tallest building anymore, the Empire State Building is certainly one of the greatest buildings in human history. The way it was designed, managed, funded, constructed, marketed, and maintained is just unique and just great. The record short time it took to build is simply miraculous given the technology of the time is was built, and even by today's most modern standards.

Many statements were made by world architects, business men, artists, professionals, celebrities, and historians trying to praise such a piece of art and glory, for example: The building was originally a symbol of hope in a country devastated by the Depression, as well as a work of accomplishment by newer immigrants. The renowned writer Benjamin Flowers states that the Empire State was "a building intended to celebrate a new America, built by men (both clients and construction workers) who were themselves new Americans." The architectural critic Jonathan Glancey refers to the building as an "icon of American design." Moreover, in a recent survey, the American Institute of Architects found that the Empire State Building was "America's favorite building."

Construction greatness is fully embodied in the story of the Empire State Building. The lessons learned from its story are just endless and enough to guide the entire construction industry today and in the future.

It highlights the powers of planning, willpower, and teamwork. I remember myself in October 2008 walking around the Empire State Building in Manhattan (Figure 3.11). I was staring at the great building from different angles with a great deal of respect and appreciation that can only be felt by a construction engineer like myself. I would hear the sounds and see the sights of the busy and high construction site, in dawns or dusks, days and nights. I also remember the long lines of hundreds of tourists and visitors from all over the world queuing up to enter the eternal building.

Figure 3.11 The author of this book looking up at the Empire State Building in 2008 AD

Story Recap Illustrated on Story Plot Diagram

The following Figure 3.12 provides an overview and recap of the story spread along the five components of the typical story telling plot diagram, namely, Exposition, Rising Action, Climax, Falling Action, and Resolution.

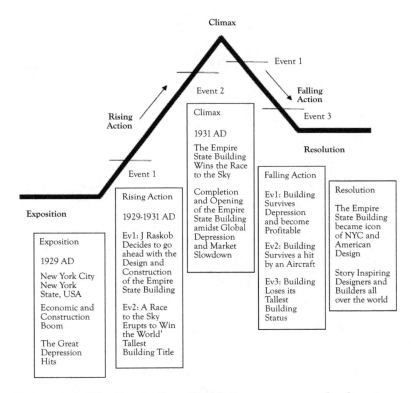

Figure 3.12 The Empire State Building story on story plot diagram

CHAPTER 4

Florence Dome, Florence, Italy— Filippo Brunelleschi and the Impossible-to-build Giant il Duomo

It's 1420 AD in Florence, Italy.

It's the year when the construction of Florence Dome started. That's 53 years after completing the dome design. The secret behind such delay was that no one knew how to build it. Renaissance architects waited for a method and the cathedral waited for a miracle. This is when Filippo Brunelleschi came up with the method and the miracle.

Figure 4.1 Florence Dome, il Duomo—Florence, Italy [1]

Table of Contents

Preface

One man in each century is given the power to achieve greatness. A mythos realized in early 1400s in Florence Italy, and the man was Filippo Brunelleschi. Filippo was just a goldsmith and clockmaker, but with a genius mind and great interest in architecture and sculpture, who was so passionate about the ancient Roman architecture. Such passion paid off so well that he himself later became a legendary master builder. The Florence Dome story began in 1296 AD with the original cathedral design completed by Arnolfo di Cambio. The design introduced a huge dome that's larger than any other dome in history. However, Arnolfo didn't tell how to design or build such a dome. In 1367 AD, Opera del Duomo got the dome designed by Neri Fioravanti, still without telling how to build it. Several attempts were made by various builders to build the giant dome; however, all failed as the scaffolding collapsed every time. In 1418 AD, Opera del Duomo called for another competition, this time to build the dome according to Neri's design, and without scaffolding. Filippo Brunelleschi placed his bid and fought for it until he won the job, however with strict conditions and controls. For 16 years, Brunelleschi had to work under enormous pressure from the skeptical public and envious rivals.

What Makes This Project Great

Florence Dome, shown in Figure 4.1, marks a turning point in the history of building and architecture and represents the glory of the Renaissance era in Europe. Moreover, the following 10 points explain why Florence Dome is great by any measure or standard:

1. The largest masonry dome ever built in the history of the world.
2. Marked the beginning of the Renaissance era with all its pride and greatness.
3. The first stone dome to be built without a supporting structure or lateral buttresses.
4. The first stone dome to use double-shell to reduce its own weight and enhance stiffness.
5. Maintained its title as the world's largest masonry dome since 1436 to the present time.
6. The dome weight is estimated at 37,000 tons and has utilized over 4 million bricks.
7. Completed with a miraculous safety record of only 3 fatalities in 16 years of construction.
8. Introduced ingenious departure from circular to balanced arched radial construction.
9. Inspired the design and construction of the dome of the famous Pantheon in Rome.
10. The diamond of the crown of Florence attracting over 10 million tourists per year.

Story Starring and Key Characters

This story is starred by all project participants, in particular the great unknown laborers and their families; without their contribution, greatness would not have been achieved.

Table 4.1 Story starring and key characters

Arnolfo Di Cambio [2]	Name	Arnolfo di Cambio
	Party	Designer of Florence Cathedral
	Title	Architect and Sculptor
	Legacy	A Florentine Architect of the early Renaissance. Arnolfo di Cambio left his mark on the style of the city of Florence. His most famous legacy is the original design of the Florence Cathedral.
	PM Role	Project Manager, Design of Cathedral
Filippo Brunelleschi [3]	Name	Filippo Brunelleschi
	Party	Design-Builder of Florence Dome
	Title	The First Renaissance Master Builder
	Legacy	A Florentine Goldsmith who won the competition to build Florence Dome and he did it miraculously and confidently. Brunelleschi is also the inventor of the geometrical system of linear perspective.
	PM Role	Project Manager, Design–Build of Dome
Lorenzo Ghiberti [4]	Name	Lorenzo Ghiberti
	Party	Supervision Consultant of Florence Dome
	Title	Goldsmith and Sculptor
	Legacy	A Florentine Goldsmith and Sculptor known as the artist of the bronze doors of the Florence Baptistery called the Gates of Paradise. His book of I Commentarii contains important writing on art.
	PM Role	Supervision Consultant, Design–Build of Dome

Arnolfo di Cambio, 1240–1310 AD, is an Italian early Renaissance Architect and Sculptor, mostly known for his outstanding original design of Florence Cathedral, Santa Maria del Fiori. In 1294–1295, he moved to and worked in Florence as an Architect and a Sculptor. In 1296, Arnolfo di Cambio developed the original design of Florence Cathedral. At a later stage, the design was perfected and completed by other Renaissance architects in the 14th and 15th centuries. However, the spectacular design of the Florence Cathedral is firmly attributed to the innovative Architect Arnolfo di Cambio. The character and elegance of Arnolfo di Cambio's work has left its flavor on the mood of the city of Florence. His funerary architecture became the model for Gothic funerary art and architecture. Arnolfo di Cambio died in 1310 AD at the age of 70 years and was buried in Florence.

Filippo Brunelleschi, 1377–1446 AD, is an Italian Renaissance Master Builder who carved his name in history for his miraculous design and construction of the legendary landmark, the Florence Dome, also known as Brunelleschi's Dome, named after Filippo Brunelleschi. Although he was basically a goldsmith, sculptor, and clockmaker, Brunelleschi was particularly interested in Architecture, especially in domes and vaults. He used to visit Rome to study and investigate the greatness of ancient Roman architecture. Thanks to his legendary Florence Dome accomplishment, Filippo Brunelleschi is considered to be an original Renaissance character and Master Builder, and the father of the Renaissance construction engineering legacy and greatness. Brunelleschi is also known for developing the "linear perspective" realistic drawing technique used in the development of perfected three-dimensional depictions of space. Filippo Brunelleschi died in 1446 AD at the age of 69 years and was buried in the Florence Cathedral, Santa Maria del Fiore.

Lorenzo Ghiberti, 1378–1455 AD, is an Italian Renaissance goldsmith, clockmaker, and artist of the early Renaissance best known for creating the bronze doors of the Florence Baptistery, called the Gates of Paradise. Ghiberti was trained as a goldsmith and sculptor and established a major metal sculpture workshop in Florence. Ghiberti first became renowned in 1401 AD when he won a competition for bronze doors, with Filippo

Brunelleschi as the second best. Ghiberti was working closely with the church in Florence for several decades and got several commissions to produce many sets of doorways with scenes from the Old Testament and the New Testament and other religious and naturalistic styles. Lorenzo Ghiberti's masterpiece however remains the bronze doors of the Florence Baptistery, dubbed by Michael Angelo as the "Gates of Paradise." The Gates of Paradise had 10 panels with 10 episodes from the Old Testament portrayed on each of them. Lorenzo Ghiberti died in 1455 AD at the age of 77 years and buried in Florence within the Santa Maria del Fiore cathedral.

4.1 Exposition: The Dome Blocking the Way to the Dream

It's the early 1400s AD in the medieval Republic of Florence, Italy. Florence is still a rural region, yet a strong rising economy and one of the wealthiest cities in Europe. Its wealth came from the wool industry, which started in the city as early as the 1200s. The finest in the world, English wool was brought to Florence to be washed in the river Arno, combed, spun and woven on timber looms, then dyed with beautiful colors. The outcome was the most expensive and most sought-after cloth in Europe, pouring money into Florence and making it wealthier by the day. With wealth and income came the desire and appetite to build, grow, and expand. That yielded a range of churches, monasteries, private palaces, as well as a 6-m-high defensive ring wall to protect the city from invaders. Gradually, the city population grew to reach 50,000, nearly the same as London's at the time, and Florence became the forefront of modernization and Renaissance in Europe. Ross King, in his book Brunelleschi's Dome, wrote: "Because of this prosperity, Florence had undergone a building boom during the 1300s the like of which had not been seen in Italy since the time of the ancient Romans. Quarries of golden-brown sandstone were opened inside the city walls; sand from the river Arno, dredged and filtered after every flood, was used in the making of mortar, and gravel was harvested from the riverbed to fill in the walls of the dozens of new buildings that had begun springing up all over the city" [King, Ross 2000]. With more wealth, prosperity, and stability came the urge to complete the construction of the giant Florence Cathedral, or Santa Maria del Fiore. In 1296, the Republic of Florence founded the Opera del Duomo body to supervise the construction of Santa Maria del Fiore, mainly funded by Florence's largest and wealthiest wool industry guild Arte della Lana. The new cathedral was meant to reflect greatness of the wealthy and ambitious Florence, and be one of utmost lavishness and glory, and when completed it was required to be more stunning and honorable than any other cathedral in the world. Forests were cut to provide timber for construction and huge slabs of marble were shipped to site along Arno River on fleets of boats. However, despite all efforts and resources, as construction progressed, more construction challenges were encountered, and the closer the cathedral came to completion, the more difficult the task appeared to be.

The original general design of Florence Cathedral was completed by the early Renaissance architect Arnolfo di Cambio in 1296 AD. Yet in 1418 AD, the cathedral was still under construction and yet to be completed. The key remaining element was the crown jewel of the entire cathedral, the element that kept architects and builders thinking for over a century. It's the missing cathedral's grand dome, as shown in Figure 4.2. An element that will later make history and serve as the crown jewel, not only of the Santa Maria del Fiore but also of Florence skyline and indeed of the entire architectural Renaissance.

Figure 4.2 Florence Cathedral without a dome, early 1400s AD [5]

Florence Cathedral's grand dome was designed to be based ca 52 m (170 ft) above ground level, and to span a diameter of ca 44 m (144 ft). That was higher and larger than any other dome built in Italy or the world at the time. Arnolfo di Cambio always intended to cover such enormous space with a dome; however, he didn't describe how to do that. The dome's architectural style was invented later on by master builder Neri di Fioravanti in a 1367 AD design competition organized by Opera del Duomo. The winning Neri di Fioravanti's dome design introduced an innovative 33 m (108 ft) high double-walled pointed rather than circular dome style, to be built without the traditional Gothic flying buttresses. That marked a major departure from traditional Gothic architecture and the beginning of the Italian Renaissance. A dome without buttresses meant the need for internal restraint and protection against spreading and outward thrust. Another key innovation was that Fioravanti's model dome was not round but a bit pointed following a quinto-acuto arch, or pointed fifth. However, Neri di Fioravanti did not engineer his innovative dome design, leaving behind a constructability challenge for future engineers and builders to resolve.

For over 50 years after Neri's dome design in 1367 AD, dome construction was either avoided for its difficulty or attempted and failed. The dome size and height simply exceeded the state-of-the-art in dome construction at the time. Several "sandstone dome" attempts were carried out by various masons and master builders; however all failed. A "concrete dome" solution akin Rome's Pantheon dome was even examined; however also deemed inappropriate as it required an enormous timber structural centering. The gross delay in completing the construction of the grand dome put the Opera del Duomo in a great embarrassment. The Republic of Florence's dream of completing their glorious cathedral seemed to be in jeopardy. On the other hand, the believers were less concerned and more confident that one day God will send the smart engineers who will be able to build the dome of their cathedral. For Opera del Duomo, it was time to wake up, stand up, and deal with the long overdue challenge. Greatness in construction appeared on the horizon of Florence, and a game-changing innovation was about to happen.

4.2 Rising Action: Greatness on the Go With Fearless Creativity

On August 19, 1418 AD, the board of the Opera del Duomo announced a nationwide competition seeking a best working solution and scale model for the construction of Neri di Fioravanti's 1367 AD dome design. The announcement read: "Whoever desires to make any model or design for the vaulting of the main Dome of the Cathedral under construction by the Opera del Duomo for armature, scaffold or other thing, or any lifting device pertaining to the construction and perfection of said cupola or vault shall do so before the end of the month of September. If the model be used he shall be entitled to a payment of 200 gold Florins." [King, Ross 2000]. Deliverables were expected to include concept drawings, scale models, and a convincing description and presentation of how the dome would be built. The assignment was prestigious, patriotic, religious, and the 200 gold Florins were quite a fortune. That attracted the attention of numerous competitors of various backgrounds from Florence and all over Tuscany. However, the competition finalists were the same two great artists who used to compete fiercely on artworks for the Baptistery, namely, Filippo Brunelleschi and Lorenzo Ghiberti. Both competitors lacked the construction experience; however, neither lacked the sharp mind, the scientific thinking, and most of all the iron unshaken willpower.

Ghiberti, the great mind trusted by the baptistery, insisted on using centering. A centering is a temporary structure made of wood used to support the stones of a dome during construction. He argued that not using centering involves a grave risk. After all, no vault or dome had ever been constructed without centering, and the dome in hand spanned 44 m, that is, larger than any other dome ever built. Ghiberti's views however were not what the jury wanted to hear; especially that Ghiberti himself was mainly an artist and didn't have enough construction experience.

Brunelleschi, on the contrary, came much better prepared than his old rival Ghiberti. He defended his proposal with passion and confidence, as depicted in Figure 4.3. On the big day, he came up with a revolutionary method to construct the dome without centering. He argued that the dome's octagonal shape designed by Neri di Fioravanti is indeed suitable and shall enable strengths not available in traditional round domes. The only two key challenges would be the stability of brick layers during construction and the strength of the entire dome after construction. Brunelleschi proposed a solution for each of the two challenges. As to brick layers stability during construction, he introduced an innovative herringbone brick-laying pattern that was validated through a model built by mason Donato di Niccolò di BettoBardi, as shown in Figure 4.4. And, regarding the overall dome strength, he proposed an innovative hoop-restrained double-shell system that would reduce dome self-weight and enhance its structural rigidity, as shown in Figure 4.8.

Figure 4.3 Brunelleschi defending his dome proposal in front of Opera del Duomo [6]

Figure 4.4 Dome brick scale model built by Donato di Niccolò di BettoBardi [7] [8]

All in all, after exhaustive debates, Filippo Brunelleschi won the fierce competition. Opera del Duomo granted him the promised 200 gold Florins prize. However, the big prize was indeed the dream assignment to build the dome and enter the history. However, the award included two risk mitigation caveats, namely: (1) Lorenzo Ghiberti to act as a capo maestro working alongside Filippo Brunelleschi; and (2) building without centering is acceptable only for the first 17.5 m, then stop and have a checkpoint for inspection before deciding on how to proceed with the remaining 14.5 m. Ghiberti's role would be supervisory, overseeing the dome construction carried out by Brunelleschi and his team on site and reporting any technical issues, risks, or failures to the client. Ghiberti was also to replace Brunelleschi as and when needed. That would give the client comfort and confidence that the project would be progressing safely and seamlessly by having a fallback plan in the case of Brunelleschi's absence, failure, sickness, or death. The 17.5 m hold point is also a remarkable management decision, since the job involved a major innovation and technological breakthrough. The decision is both wise to ensure that Brunelleschi is indeed in control of the operations according to his assumptions and promises, as well as to address Ghiberti's grave concerns expressed during the dome competition when he stated that the dome could not be built without centering.

In 1420 AD, construction of the dome started after all awards and funding arrangements were made. Brunelleschi was faced with a number of major design and construction challenges. Design challenges were mainly structural and directly linked to construction and constructability. Structural challenges had to do with identifying and resisting internal and external forces and stresses in the dome shell. These are typically generated by dead loads such as self-weight, external tiles, and the lantern, and live loads such as earthquakes, snow loads, and wind load. Domes shells respond to loads in ways that are similar to arches, except that arches require external lateral restraint, whereas domes can be stabilized externally or internally through reinforcing the dome hoops and meridians. Hoops work in horizontal planes, whereas meridians work in vertical panes. Failure of hoops under tensile forces results in vertical cracking in the dome shell, whereas failure of meridians under compressive forces can result in dome shell bulging and downward collapse.

As such, Brunelleschi had to provide in-shell hoops and meridians to maintain the structural integrity, resist internal structural stresses, and prevent formation of cracks. To that end, and as shown in Figure 4.8, he embedded parallel chains of sandstone and timber to take up hoop tensile forces and prevent cracking, and rigid vertical sandstone ribs at the lines between the octagonal dome's eight faces to take up meridian forces and avoid bulging. Brunelleschi did not have structural engineering training, but he had the accuracy of a clockmaker, his original profession. As is expected to manage the risk of innovation, Brunelleschi surrounds himself with a strong team of top talents. That included highly skilled masons, surveyors, carpenters, sandstone makers, smiths, and machine builders. Brunelleschi's key role was to provide technical input, orchestrate the efforts, in addition to setting out the works and inventing the stones lifting devices. Setting out the octagonal dome works was a complex task

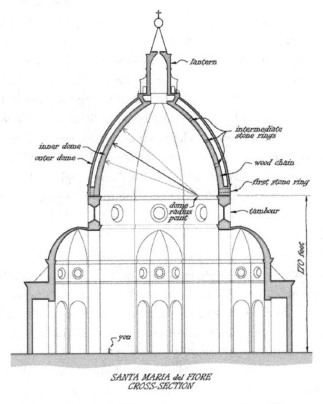

Figure 4.5 Santa Maria del Fiore dome cross-section [9]

for which Brunelleschi invented a system of central axis and radial ropes to ensure that all eight walls shall meet accurately at the top of the dome.

As shown in Figures 4.5 and 4.8, the dome structure consisted of the following structural elements, which acted together as a whole one forming a stable dome that will pass the test of time and remain intact for over 600 years defying aging and straining actions:

1. Dome-Base Sandstone Chain Hoop: A sturdy nonelastic sandstone chain hoop was embodied in the octagonal dome-base, resting upon the tambour structure. Hoop is responsible to resist the radial outward forces taking place at the basis of the dome. Rigidity is absolutely important at this location to ensure that no or absolutely minimal deformation strains are transferred to the underlain tambour structure. The dome-base is ca 170 ft above the floor level. The sandstone chain hoop system looked like a railroad-rack with two main sandstone beams connected longitudinally with iron clamps and laterally with sandstone cross beams fitted in notches made in the bottom of the sandstone beams, as shown in Figure 4.8.

2. The Inner Shell: The thicker shell of the double-shelled dome. The shell is 2.20-m thick and was made of strong sand stones for the first 7 m, then of lightweight clay bricks until the top. That was key to reduce the dome self-weight near the center, especially that there was no centering. The inner shell depended in its stability during and after construction on the use of the herringbone brick-laying pattern invented by Brunelleschi. The spiral herringbone pattern shown in Figure 4.8 prevented bricks from sliding during laying when mortar is wet, and averted the weak shear planes between brick layers through the vertical brick elements. The vertical ribs created between the eight faces of the octagonal dome also enhanced dome stability and strength. As shown in Figure 4.8, the inner shell was reinforced with one timber hoop and three sandstone hoops along its height, which helped giving the dome stability and structural integrity.

3. The Outer Shell: The thicker shell of the double-shelled dome receiving the external loads such as wind, snow, and temperature. The outer shell was 0.80-m thick at the base reducing gradually to 0.30 m

at the top and was made of clay bricks. The outer shell did not have hoops and was just fortified by the herringbone brick-laying patterns and corner ribs. The inner and outer shells were separated by 1.20 m (4 ft) cavity and connected by ribs and offshoot links. The 4-m-deep hollow innovative cross section formed by the two shells (2.20 m inner shell + 1.20 m void + 0.80 m outer shell) provided an effective structural system of reduced self-weight and higher dome shell sectional lever arm to resist structural stresses.

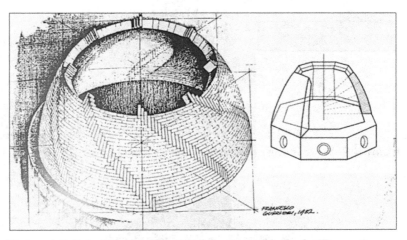

Figure 4.6 Spiral herringbone brick-laying method—by Francesco Gurrieri 1982 [10]

A key challenge faced during construction was lifting and lowering the heavy stones and construction materials. That had to be done in a controlled-motion way for the safety of the works and the workers. To that end, Brunelleschi invented a unique hoisting device base on the innovative reverse-gear mechanism, as shown in Figure 4.7. While horses or oxen were turning in the same direction, by a shift of a gear, stones and weights were able to travel either up or down the device shaft, as desired. This genius invention involving the creative use of gears probably had to do with Brunelleschi's background as a clockmaker. Only three fatal site accidents reported over the many years of construction, which is an astonishingly good safety record. The job was the accurate and precise installation of 4 million bricks. That's about 800 bricks per working day assuming a site calendar of 6 working days per week.

Figure 4.7 Stone lifting device with reverse gear [11]

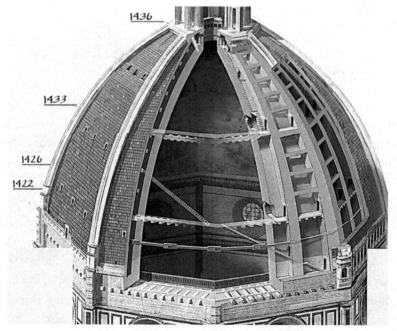

Figure 4.8 Florence Dome structural system and rate of progress [12]

The construction of the Florence dome took about 16 years to complete. Throughout such duration, Brunelleschi had to work under pressure from negative stakeholders who did not want him to succeed or did not believe he would succeed. These included his lifetime rival Lorenzo Ghiberti who was commissioned to supervise the project, the public who were fearful of a catastrophic failure, and even the client who did not really like him. Brunelleschi, however, turned these negativities to his and the project's advantage. That's by excelling in each step and leaving no chance for failure. The safe and controlled construction completion of the Florence dome, without centering, was a major technological triumph. The impossible became a reality and the whole world applauded.

4.3 Climax: Project Completion and Celebration

On March 25, 1436 AD, the Santa Maria del Fiore Cathedral was inaugurated by Pope Eugene IV, the head of the Catholic Church and ruler of the Papal States. During the inauguration ceremony, Guillaume Dufay's masterpiece of music titled "Nuper Rosarum Flores" in Latin, or "Recently Blossomed the Flowers" in English, was played (music available on YouTube). The piece was composed for the occasion, and its name stems from the name of the grand cathedral, Santa Maria del Fiore. It's a moment of greatness and pride. A long-awaited moment for Florence and the Florentines. A major objective that took the nation 140 years to achieve. That is, from 1296 AD, when the cathedral was first designed by Arnolfo Di Cambio, all the way down to this moment, in 1436 AD. Now, Florence can rest. Now, the Florence Dome is finally in place. Like a hat to bare head, or a jewel to a jewel-less crown. A major achievement that attracted the attention of world and gave the construction industry at the time a much-needed moral boost. When completed in 1436 AD, the iconic cathedral dome was the largest stone dome in the world, and continued to maintain this status until the present time. The Florence Dome marked the beginning of the Renaissance in Europe and gave the whole region a whole new spirit or hope and confidence. Glory to Filippo Brunelleschi and his team for the pride, inspiration, and honor they brought to the civil engineering profession and professionals all over the world.

4.4 Falling Action: More Beauty and More Cracks

After the completion of the dome, came a period of pleasure and prosperity. Florence Dome attracted a lot of attention in Europe and the world as an iconic landmark, an engineering miracle, and the largest dome in the world. Although the cathedral was fully operational on the day of inauguration, something was missing. It's the dome lantern. It will be added a decade later, adding beauty, height, and greatness. Opera del Duomo held another competition for the design and construction of the lantern, which Brunelleschi again won. This time for his compelling design, as well as rock solid credibility and full familiarity with the dome itself. In fact, Brunelleschi had always had the Lantern in mind while building the dome, and made some provisions to incorporate it at a later stage. Construction of the Lantern began a few months before Brunelleschi's death in 1444 AD. Work was continued and completed by Brunelleschi's friend Michelozzo di Bartolommeo. The installation of the Lantern increased the height of the dome to 114.5 m (376 ft), making it one of the highest buildings in the world at the time. The Lantern also added to the dome a great deal of character and beauty, pride and greatness.

Almost 600 years after construction, the dome has been intact, behaving great and taking the blows with pride and greatness. Blows included cycles of freezing winters and burning summers, earthquakes, snow loads, wind loads, and loads of the people climbing the stairs located in between the outer and inner shells up to the dome observation deck. However, as with all creatures of all kinds, aging is inevitable, and some cracks started to appear and propagate in the body of the dome. The first survey of dome cracks took place as early as the 16th century, then a similar condition survey almost every century thereafter. A late 20th-century report indicated the presence of ca 500 cracks of various sizes and widths widening to up to 3 mm in winter and less in summer (Suro, Reberto 1987). These cracks are however not so serious, structurally, and may only indicate that the dome is breathing. After all, all buildings breathe.

4.5 Resolution: Florence Dome Today

Today, the Florence Dome, best known as il Duomo, is the largest stone dome in the world forming highly recognizable feature on the world skyline, as shown in Figure 4.9. It also embodies a structural engineering wonder that's still keeping engineers pondering, how it was built without centering, and how it really works. That's despite the current 21st century's technological advancement in terms of computer-aided structural design and advanced construction equipment. Florence Dome brings to the viewer's mind the essence and powers of the great Renaissance era. The powers of fearless innovation, effective planning, and confident use of brain power and engineering principles to tackle complex construction issues. Today, the Florence Dome is highly honored on the world stage and listed with UNESCO as a World Heritage Site. The Florentines are still holding a parade every year in the streets of Florence to honor and commemorate the genius Filippo Brunelleschi.

Figure 4.9 Recent Aerial view of Florence Cathedral by Bruce Stokes [13]

Story Recap Illustrated on Story Plot Diagram

The following Figure 4.10 provides an overview and recap of the story spread along the five components of the typical story telling plot diagram, namely, Exposition, Rising Action, Climax, Falling Action, and Resolution.

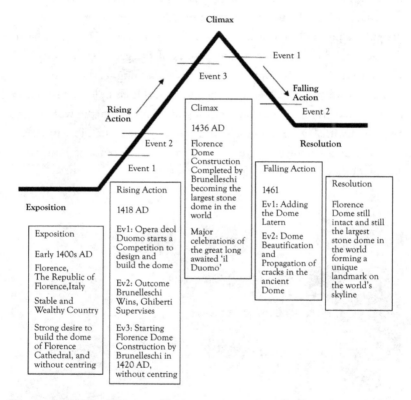

Figure 4.10 The Florence Dome story on story plot diagram

CHAPTER 5

The Eiffel Tower, Paris, France— Gustave Eiffel and The Ironwork Monster that Turned into a Symbol of Love

It's the mid 1880's AD in Paris, France.

France is getting ready to celebrate the first centennial of its great revolution. The celebration had to be great and planned to host the 1889 AD World Fair. The World Fair monument had to be great. As great as France's history, and as high as France's profile and ambitions. That was the Eiffel Tower.

Figure 5.1 Eiffel Tower, Paris, France [1]

Table of Contents

Preface

Greatness made of iron. Made of confidence, pride, passion, and beauty. This is story of the legendary Eiffel Tower, shown in Figure 5.1, born in Paris, France in 1889 AD. Born to bring joy to life, and symbolize values of love, elegance, and freedom. The story began in 1884 AD with the French government's decision to celebrate the centennial of the French Revolution, due in 1889 AD. In 1886 AD, Gustave Eiffel, the brilliant French contractor, won a national competition to design a monument to support the World's Fair to be held in Paris in the same year of the centennial. The monument had to be as great as the French Revolution itself. Amidst opposition from haters and critiques, Gustave Eiffel and his brilliant team began the tower design and construction in early 1887 AD. When completed, the giant 324 m (1063 ft) high Eiffel Tower broke the world record becoming the tallest structure in the world, almost double the height of the Washington Monument. Greatness was felt in the air in the Camps de Mars Park where the tower was built, all over Paris, and indeed all over the world. The seductive ironwork tower standing on the verge of La Seine River in Paris has become a world's "Symbol of Love," and romance.

What Makes This Project Great

The Eiffel Tower marks a turning point in the history of building and architecture and represents a glorifying "output product" of the Industrial Revolution. Moreover, the following 10 points explain why the Eiffel Tower is great by any measure or standard:

1. One of the most iconic man-made monuments in the world.
2. The highest observation deck in Europe at 276 m (906 ft) high.
3. The tallest tower in the world at the time it was built, 324 m (1,063 ft) high.
4. Considered by some groups to be one of the top if not the Seven Wonders of the World.
5. Pioneered-basing construction on structural analysis and design calculations.
6. Sets perfect example for the application of the design–build method in the recent history.
7. The world's oldest known example for the application of the PPP and BOOT contracts.
8. One of the world's most visited touristic landmarks with ca 7 million visitors a year.
9. Tower construction utilized ca 7,500 tons of ironwork and 2.5 million connection rivets.
10. Completed in record design–build time of 26 months, that is 2 years, 2 months, and 5 days.

Story Starring and Key Characters

This story is starred by all project participants, in particular the great unknown laborers and their families; without their contribution, greatness would not have been achieved.

Table 5.1 Story starring and key characters

Gustave Eiffel [2]	Name	**Gustave Eiffel**
	Party	Compagnie des Établissements Eiffel
	Title	Managing Director
	Legacy	A French tycoon and Ironwork Constructor. A symbol of the Industrial Revolution. Best known for his iconic Eiffel Tower in Paris and fabricating the structure of the Statue of Liberty in New York.
	PM Role	Project Sponsor, Design and Construction
Maurice Koechlin [3]	Name	**Maurice Koechlin**
	Party	Compagnie des Établissements Eiffel
	Title	Chief Structural Engineer
	Legacy	A Franco–Swiss Civil and Structural Engineer who excelled in innovative designs of ironwork structures including concept and structural design of Eiffel Tower, Garabit Viaduct, and Statue of Liberty.
	PM Role	Project Manager, Design and Construction
Stephen Sauvestre [4]	Name	**Stephen Sauvestre**
	Party	Compagnie des Établissements Eiffel
	Title	Head of Architectural Department
	Legacy	A French Architect who played a key role in the decoration and beautification of the Eiffel Tower. He worked closely with Gustave Eiffel and Civil Engineers Maurine Koechlin and Emile Nouguier.
	PM Role	Project Architect, Design and Construction

Gustave Eiffel, 1832–1923 AD, a French chemist, ironwork contractor, businessman, and scientific researcher. In 1855 AD, he graduated from École Centrale des Arts et Manufactures of France specializing in chemistry. After graduation, he got trained and sponsored by the railway engineer Charles Nepveu who helped him get his first job designing a small bridge for the Saint Germaine railway. In 1866 AD, he established his own ironwork workshop and got his first important project to design and build two bridge viaducts for the railway line between Lyon and Bordeaux. In 1868 AD, he entered into partnership with the contractor Théophile Seyrig and they jointly completed many projects. In 1879 AD, his partnership with Seyrig was dissolved and Gustave Eiffel established his own company Compagnie des Établissements Eiffel, which will later build the Eiffel Tower and Statue of Liberty. In 1893 AD, he retired and devoted the rest of his life to scientific research looking into wind pressure behavior, meteorology, and aerodynamics. In 1923 AD, Gustave died at the age of 91 years in his mansion in Paris.

Maurice Koechlin, 1856–1946 AD, a Franco-Swiss structural engineer best known for structural design and engineering of Eiffel Tower, in association with his colleague Emile Nouguier. In 1877 AD, Maurice graduated from the Polytechnikum Zürich with a degree in Civil Engineering. He then started his career working for the French railway company "Chemin de Fer de l'Est" for two years. In 1879 AD, he joined Gustav Eiffel's company the Compagnie des Établissements Eiffel, with which he completed numerous remarkable ironwork structures. In 1887 AD, he took the lead on developing the shape and concept of the unique Eiffel Tower as well as in finalizing its structural calculations and construction details. In 1893 AD, Maurice Koechlin became the managing director of the Compagnie des Établissements Eiffel after retirement of Gustave Eiffel. Maurice Koechlin died in 1946 AD at the age of 80 in his house in Switzerland.

Stephen Sauvestre, 1847–1919 AD, a French architect and artist. In 1868 AD, he graduated from ÉcoleSpécialed' Architecture in France. At time of the Eiffel Tower design and construction, he was the Head of the Architecture Department at Compagnie des Établissements Eiffel. When the structural engineers Maurice Koechlin and Emile Nouguier presented the tower's conceptual sketch he didn't entirely like it, and requested further study. This is when Stephen Sauvestre got involved by introducing a range of artistic details and effects to the sketch including decorative arches to the tower base, the glass pavilion to the tower's first level, the tower top cupola, and later on the tower's brilliant color scheme of the tower. Credit goes to the talented Architect Stephen Sauvestre for the beauty of the Eiffel Tower decorative details we all see today and which keep visitors gazing at the tower for hours. Stephen Sauvestre died in 1919 AD at the age of 72.

5.1 Exposition: French Revolution Inspires a Design Revolution

It's the 14th of July 1789 AD in Paris, France. The angry rebels storming the Bastille causing a flashpoint that will ignite the French Revolution. A great event that changed the face of France and marked the end of the medieval monarchies and the beginning of an era of modern republics and liberal democracies. A little less than hundred years later, France was getting ready to celebrate the centennial memorial of its great revolution. In the meantime, the French economy was suffering. The nation was in a critical need for an economic boost and a lift of spirits. To that end, the French leaders decided to take the opportunity of the revolution's centennial in 1889 AD and host a World Fair. Arrangements started slowly in the mid-1880s AD with many ideas put on the table for how to impress the world on that day. As is common in World Fairs, there was a need for an iconic centerpiece monument to represent the major event. Monument was to reflect status, strength, and stability of the hosting country. Great ambitions call for a great monument, and France's ambitions and sense of patriotism and national pride were greater than ever.

In 1884 AD, Gustave Eiffel and his Compagnie des Établissements Eiffel, being a key ironwork structures contractor in Paris, decided to participate in this strategic national effort. He entrusted his brilliant chief structural engineer Maurice Koechlin to look into the matter and propose a concept. The monument needed to reflect France's greatness, status, and sky high ambitions. In May 1884, Maurice Koechlin presented an initial sketch to Gustave Eiffel as shown in Figure 5.2. The sketch looked very much like the finally built tower; however, was rough and purely structural. A four-legged metal truss girders ironwork tower, wide at the base and gets symmetrically narrower on all four corners in a curved path as the tower goes high, ending with a tip point. Gustave Eiffel didn't like the design in the first instance; however, didn't reject it and requested further study and details. The structural engineers took the sketch to the head of architectural department, Stephen Sauvestre, asking him for input, opinion, and support. Stephen Sauvestre added beauty and features to the structural sketch including decorative arches and features to the base, a glass pavilion to the first level, and the prominent tower cupola to the top of the tower. In addition, he introduces the brilliant color scheme of the tower with dark blue in lower levels and lighter blue at higher levels to match Paris skyline. Gustave Eiffel approved the final conceptual sketches and bought the patent rights of the design developed by Marcus Koechlin, Emile Nouguier, and Stephen Sauvestre.

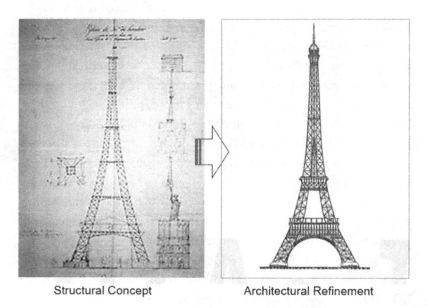

Structural Concept   Architectural Refinement

Figure 5.2 Maurice Koechlin's initial sketch of Eiffel Tower [5] [6]

In March 1885 AD, Gustave Eiffel presented his proposed monument design to the Société des Ingénieurs Civils (The Society of Civil Engineer) discussing technical features and challenges, while labeling the monument as an expression of France's gratitude. That was an excellent proactive step to make the patented design known to the highest technical body in France and to the civil engineering community. Still, moving the matter forward required a political will at the highest level, and certainly availing the required funds. That happened in 1886 with the re-election of Jules Grévy as president of France and the appointment of Édouard Lockroy as the minister of Trade. A budget was allocated for the construction of the World Fair monument. On May 01, 1886 AD, the new minister announced an open competition for the World Fair 1889 AD centerpiece monument. Tower location was tentatively planned to take place somewhere in the Champ de Mars park in Paris. A competent technical commission was set up to examine and select the winning best monument design. The owner requirements and monument success criteria were defined as a 300 m (984 ft) high four-sided metal tower, which was kind of tailored to accept Gustave Eiffel's proposal. In June 1886 AD, the commission decided that none of the proposals were acceptable, except Gustave Eiffel's proposal. In January 1887 AD, Gustave Eiffel signed a contract with the government to complete the design and construction of the tower before the 1889 AD World Fair opening date. The contract was akin the modern PPP Public Private Partnership or BOOT Build Own Operate Transfer contracts. The deal was that the French government pays Gustave Eiffel a sum of 1.5 million Francs (French currency at the time) out of the tower's estimated cost of 6.5 million Francs; on the other hand, Gustave Eiffel gets the right for the commercial exploitation of the tower for 20 years. The tower was located at the Entrance of the World's Fair in a strategic spot within the Champs De Mars Park close to the verge of the Seine River, as shown in Figure 5.3. So the deal was done and clock started ticking.

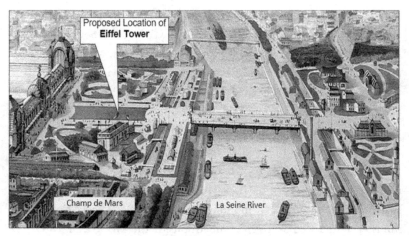

Figure 5.3 Proposed location of Eiffel Tower in Champ de Mars [7]

5.2 Rising Action: Greatness on the Go With Fearless Creativity

In January 1887 AD, Gustave Eiffel and his team proceeded with the tower structural design, in parallel with site preparation and subsoil investigation. The key structural design challenge was to evaluate and resist wind loads under the worst anticipated wind gust, in addition to live loads, temperature, and self-weight. That task constituted a major technological breakthrough. The proposed Eiffel Tower was ca 324 m (1,063 ft) high, whereas the tallest man-made monument in the world at the time, the Washington Monument, was merely 169 m (555 ft) high. The tower base was squared, four legged, of about 125 m each side. The tower was located at the Entrance of the World's Fair next to the Seine River. The tower legs were diagonally almost pointing North–South and East–West. Figure 5.4 shows the Eiffel Tower's general arrangement and key dimensions.

The attractive yet optimized tower shape and curvatures offered most effective efficient aerodynamics for the best wind resistance possible. The power of architectural design by structural engineers. Structural design used simple linear elastic analysis in which forces in members are calculated based on statically determinate systems and graphical methods. The tower's structural system consisted of main members made of box sections connected with lattices and trusses made of angle sections or flat plates. The ultimate stress of the iron used was about 300 MPa. A safety coefficient of at least 2.5 on the ultimate tensile strength. The wind effects were

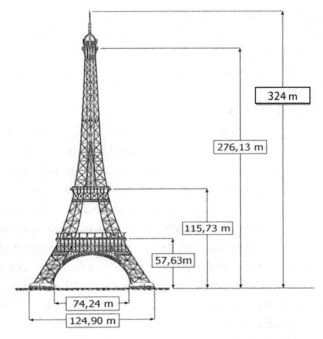

Figure 5.4 Eiffel Tower general arrangement and key dimensions [6]

evaluated and the tower was examined for two assumed loading scenarios: (1) A wind pressure of 2.000 N/m² constant to the 2nd floor and then varying linearly to 4.000 N/m² at the top of the tower; and (2) A wind pressure of 1.000 N/m² at the basement increasing linearly to 3.000 N/m² at the top of the tower. For the temperature loads and effects, a range of -30°C/+30°C uniform throughout the tower was used. All structural elements were designed to be firm and compact with a relatively low slenderness ratio less of than 45 for the main members and 40 for the bracing members (Rondal 2006). The ironwork design and engineering task was a tedious exercise and a wonder in itself. Marcus Koechlin and his team did a great job behind the scene to make things happen on site. That included structural analysis, structural design, and ironwork members, dimensioning, and high precision fabrication and erection drawings. The project design office consisted of 50 engineers (SETE 2020) and produced 1,700 general arrangement drawings and 3,629 detailed ironwork drawings of the 18,038 different parts needed to build the giant tower (Loyrette 1985). The design, engineering, and drawings production tasks were key to project success. They involved a high level of sophistication and excellence that truly reflected Gustave Eiffel's way of innovating and having a scientific basis to each step of the construction process. Indeed, this was the way and spirit of the second industrial revolution best, represented by Gustave Eiffel.

On January 28, 1887 AD, excavation for the foundation works started. That's a short time after signing the contract, which took place earlier in the month. The task to build a solid foundation that can take the tower foundation loads safely with minimal settlement and/or differential settlement. To that end, an in-depth subsoil investigation and analysis was conducted to study soil properties and decide suitable foundation depth, size, and system. Luckily, the subsoil was hard enough, however required 15 m (50 ft) excavation to remove the weak topsoil and base the foundations on the hard strata. The tower had four legs, so required four foundation footings, each consisting of a 6 m (20 ft) deep concrete slab. Moreover, the two footings running parallel to the Seine River were further supported with deep foundation caissons. Atop the four concrete slabs footings a block of cement-bounded limestone bricks was installed with inclined top face to accommodate the anchor bolts required to connect the tower metal legs ironwork shoes to the foundation footing, as shown in Figure 5.6. Each ironwork shoe was connected to the stonework by a pair of anchor bolts 10 cm (4 inch) diameter and 5.5 m (25 ft) long. On June 30, 1987 AD, the foundation works were completed, and the erection of the tower superstructure ironwork began July 1, 1887 AD, as shown in Figure 5.5.

Ironically, while the tower construction was ramping up getting well underway, loud opposition protests against its construction were going on in Paris. Opposition was led by the prominent architect Charles Garnier and included numerous Parisian architects, artists, and sculptures who formed a body called "Committee of the 324," referring to the tower's 324-m height, to protest against the construction of the tower trying to stop from happening. The opposition's point of view was that aesthetically, the tower looks extremely odd, just like a gigantic black smokestack, and that would overshadow Paris's most treasured cultural buildings such as Notre Dame, Le Louvre, and the Arc de Triomphe. Gustave Eiffel, however, was not so concerned about such opposition and responded by

Figure 5.5 Eiffel Tower foundation and beginning of ironwork erection [8]

arguing that they have to wait until the tower is built to make a fair judgment, that the tower located in Cham de Mars par is indeed far away from the buildings they are afraid it might overwhelm, and that the tower when completed will be a great grandiose just like Egypt's Pyramids, except it will be much higher than the pyramids and that it will indeed be the highest man-made building in the world.

While the tower foundations were being designed and built, tower ironwork was being designed, fabricated, and prepared for shipping to site once the foundations were completed. The production and erection of the tower components was an extremely difficult exercise due to the complex angles involved in the design. It required exceptionally high fabrication accuracy and a fabrication tolerance as low as 1 mm (0.04 in) for positioning of rivet holes. Ironwork fabrication was carried out at a factory owned by Gustave Eiffel located in the nearby Parisian suburb of Levallois-Perret. To facilitate and expedite erection, parts of the tower were riveted together into subassemblies, shipped from the factory to the site on horse-drawn carts. They were first bolted together at the factory, then the bolts were replaced with rivets on site after alignment and positioning were confirmed, as construction progressed. No drilling or shaping was done on site. If any part did not fit, it was sent back to the factory for alteration. In all, the tower design and construction involved 50 engineers and designers, 150 fabrication workers at the fabrication factory, and 324 tower assembly workers on site. The tower structure involved 7,500 tons of iron in the form of 18,038 pieces joined and assembled together using 2.5 million rivets [SETE 2020]. The assembly of the innovative breakthrough tower required extremely advanced skills and creativity. For that challenging, and indeed historical task, Gustave Eiffel appointed his trusted man and ironwork erection guru Mr. Jean Compagnon, the company's chief assembling manager. Jean Compagnon developed and deployed a range of tremendously sophisticated and innovative propping and alignment systems and devices to cater for the tower's 3D curving body, which required a high level of accuracy and imagination combined with very low fabrication tolerance. In recognition of the successful completion of the historical tower assembly, Jean Compagnon was granted the highest French award of "Knight of the Legion of Honor."

Assembling the tower took place in four main stages, namely, the First Stage including the tower base block extending from the tower foundation up to the first level, almost 57-m high, the Second Stage extending up to the second level almost 115-m high, achieving a significant reduction of the tower width and bulk, the Third Stage which extended up to the third level, almost 195-m high, and the Fourth and final Stage extending to the tower's final height of 324 m including the tower top cupola.

Even when the structural works of the tower were successfully completed, many Parisian engineers remained skeptical about the tower's design. They accused Gustave Eiffel and his team of trying to impress and get artistic without giving due consideration to the principles of physics and structural engineering. In particular, they questioned the sky-high tower's capacity in resisting wind loads. Gustave Eiffel dismissed such charges explaining that his experienced bridge builders have indeed realized the importance of wind forces, assessed them, and took them into account while designing the tower. After all, the tower constituted a major structural engineering breakthrough and was going to be the tallest structure in the world. The tower structural design team used graphical methods to determine the forces in the tower members and connections resulting from wind loads, rather than mathematical formulae. All parts of the tower were designed to cater for maximum anticipated wind forces with adequate safety factor. The tower sways by up to 9 cm (3.5 in) under maximum wind, which is a small value given the tower's 324-m height. It indicates the existence of low stress levels in the tower truss members, thanks to its genius shape getting narrower as the tower goes higher. Tower construction was completed safely and the end product was an incredible iron monster penetrating the cloudy skies of Paris and the world.

5.3 Climax: Project Completion and Celebration

On March 31, 1889 AD, Gustave Eiffel led a group of government officials, representatives of the press, and a host of this tower team on a guided tour to the top of the tower, as shown in Figure 5.6. As the tower passengers' lifts were not installed yet at this point, the mounting had to be by foot, a tiresome stair-climbing journey of over an hour. Most of the delegation couldn't make it on the stairs to the 276 m (906 ft) high top observation deck. Only a few made it including the structural engineer, Émile Nouguier; the head of construction and tower assembly, Jean Compagnon; the President of the City Council; and some reporters from Le Figaro and Le Monde Illustré. At 2:35 pm, Gustave Eiffel rose a large flag of France complemented with of a 25-gun salute fired at the first observation level (Harvie 2006). On the same day's night, the glorious tower was further celebrated by lighting hundreds of gas lamps and a giant beacon casting out three beams of the French flag colors, red, white, and blue.

It was a day to remember, a dream come true, a technological breakthrough, and a major achievement of the French nation that will last for centuries thereafter and attract hundreds of millions of visitors and admirers from all over the world. Most importantly at the time, the tower perfectly served its initial purpose as the main exhibit at the 1889 Exposition Universelle (World's Fair), which was held to mark and celebrate the centennial of the French Revolution that took place in 1789. The spectacular success of the tower design and construction and its breathtaking greatness and attractiveness silenced Gustave Eiffel's critiques and made

Figure 5.6 Inauguration of the Eiffel Tower on March 31,
1889 AD [9]

the whole world think. The tower achieved immediate popularity success
with nearly 30,000 visitors who decided to take the 1,710 steps climbing
to the top of the tower before the two passengers lifts were completely
fitted and made operational on May 26, 1889 AD. By the end of the
exposition, the number of the visitors to the Eiffel Tower rose to a record
high number of nearly 1.9 million. The great Eiffel Tower, the highest
tower in the world at the time, changed the skyline of Paris, of France,
and indeed of the entire world forever.

5.4 Falling Action: Continued Pride, Passion, and Elegance

The tower was originally planned to stay for only 20 years then
dismantled; however, it has survived to date in complete pride and tact.
Shortly after tower completion, Gustave Eiffel quit construction and
devoted the rest of his career to scientific research of wind loads and
aerodynamics. Many actions and events and nonstructural modifications

happened to the tower since its completion and inauguration on March 1889 AD. In 1900 AD, the lifts in the east and west legs were replaced by lifts running as far as the second observation deck level. At the same time, the lift in the north pillar was removed and replaced by a staircase to the first level. In 1930 AD, the tower lost the title of the world's tallest structure when the Chrysler Building in New York City was completed. In 1935 AD, the tower was used for experimental low-resolution television transmissions. In 1940 AD, when the German troops invaded Paris, the French cut the passenger lift cables to prevent the troops from climbing the tower. In 1944 AD, the German leader Adolf Hitler visited Paris, stopped by the tower, but chose to stay on the ground, and ordered the demolition of the tower, an order that was never honored. Later in the year 1944 AD, the German troops were driven out of Paris, and the German flag atop the Eiffel Tower was replaced with the French Flag. Figure 5.7 presents a photo of the American soldiers passing by the Eiffel Tower and saluting the French flag flying on the Eiffel Tower after freeing Paris.

Figure 5.7 American soldiers saluting the French Flag Eiffel Tower in 1944 AD [10]

In 1956, a fire erupted in the television transmitter damaging the top of the tower. In 1964, the Eiffel Tower was officially declared to be a historical monument by the Minister of Cultural Affairs, André Malraux. In 2002 AD, the tower marked its 200 million visitors' line. In 2003 AD, the tower had operated at its maximum capacity of about 7 million visitors per year. In 2004 AD, the Eiffel Tower began hosting a seasonal ice rink on the first level. In 2014 AD, the Eiffel Tower saw a refurbishment effort that included a glass floor on its first level. Otherwise, no significant tower structural defects or anomalies were reported and the Eiffel Tower stood sturdy and proud as elegant as on its day of inauguration.

5.5 Resolution: The Eiffel Tower Today

Today, many decades after its construction, the elegant Eiffel Tower is still standing sturdy and strong, unshaken by the years, the weather, the wind, the frost, or the earthquakes. In theory, the iron tower can last for thousands of years if it could resist its two main natural aging enemies, namely, corrosion and fatigue. Corrosion is caused by water and air that can oxidize and weaken iron in the long term, if it is left bare and uncovered by a suitable corrosion protection paint. The protective paint coating can protect the metal from corrosion; however, it must be renewed periodically. In fact, the tower is being repainted every seven years or so, which appears to be a reasonable frequency for the size of the tower and the current state of technology in the field of protective coatings. So if repainted and protected properly against corrosion, the tower can theoretically last for a very long time. The other natural aging enemy of the tower is the fatigue effect. Fatigue effect is a physical phenomenon that can weaken metals or other materials due to repeated cyclical stresses even of small magnitudes. In the case of the Eiffel Tower, such cyclical low magnitude stresses are mainly caused by wind and temperature. Wind loads can cause large numbers of stress cycles manifested in tower deflections and slight vibrations. Temperature changes between night and day can also cause a large number of stress cycles manifested in the metal tower's expansions and contractions. Temperature change stresses and strains over a 24-hour day and night period can cause a tower tip circular movement of a diameter of ca 6 in (15 cm). These cyclic small movements and stresses can cause the metal to fatigue in the long term. That's similar to folding a metal or plastic plate many times until it breaks. However, given the slim and sturdy tower design and the safety factor embedded into dimensioning of its iron member, a failure due to fatigue also needs a very long time to occur. Another advantage of the genius lattice-like design of the tower is that a defective tower component could be replaced without affecting the tower's shape or stability.

The Eiffel Tower currently ranks 31st on the list of the highest structures in the world, after being on the top of the list in 1889 AD. However, its impact and attractiveness is certainly still high on the top of the list. The tower embodies extraordinary value, legacy, and prestige on the world stage, so it is far more than just a tall tower. Eiffel Tower made history when completed in 1889 AD, and is still making a buzz many years after its construction. Moreover, history will always remember that the Eiffel Tower is the first man-made building in the human history to surpass the 324-m height line. The attractive landmark is now receiving ca 7 million visitors a year, which is the tower's maximum visiting capacity. The actual number of tourists visiting Paris to see the tower is certainly way higher than this number. For many people in the world, the seductive Eiffel Tower, standing on the verge of La Seine River, has become a "Symbol of Love" and romance. Some even visualize it as a lady, and call it in French "La Dame de Fer," or the iron lady. Moreover, the Eiffel Tower, since its inauguration, has become a major source of income to France through tourism, entertainment, and advertisement. Indeed, it also became a major source of the French national pride and prestige. Credit goes to the genius Gustave Eiffel, and his great Eiffel Tower team who made history and left behind them a legacy and a pride of France in particular and of the construction profession at large.

Story Recap Illustrated on Story Plot Diagram

The following Figure 5.8 provides an overview and recap of the story spread along the five components of the typical story telling plot diagram, namely, Exposition, Rising Action, Climax, Falling Action, and Resolution.

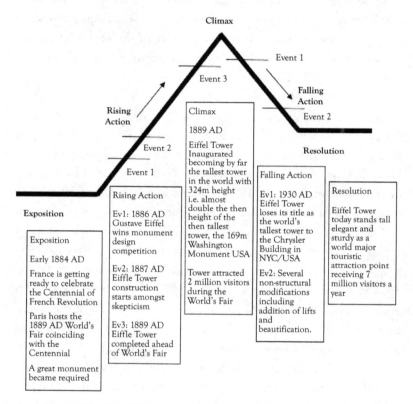

Figure 5.8 The Eiffel Tower story on story plot diagram

CHAPTER 6

New Al Gourna Village, Luxor, Egypt—Architect Hassan Fathy and the Story of the Doomed Domed Mud Palaces

It's 1946 AD in Luxor, Egypt.

A royal decree is issued to relocate Al Gourna village resting atop a major pharaonic archeological site. Hassan Fathy took over the mission and built a great new village. The universe loved the new village, and nature celebrated the birth of Green Architecture. All good and fine, however, a big surprise was waiting for Hassan Fathy.

Figure 6.1 The doomed domed mud palaces of New Al Gourna [1]

Table of Contents

Preface

Greatness in construction can be achieved through great buildings. It can also be achieved through great noble causes and moral drives. This is embodied in the story of New Al Gourna village. A project masterminded by the Egyptian Architect Hassan Fathy who believed that poor folks deserve to live in palaces, even if such palaces are just made of mud, as shown in Figure 6.1. To Hassan Fathy, people's life style, heath, and behaviors can be improved through architecture while maintaining heritage. That's like changing an outfit from rutting old to elegant new without changing the style or dress culture. The story began in 1946 AD with a Royal Decree to relocate the Gourna village sitting atop a major pharaonic necropolis, the Tomb of the Nobles. Among several candidates, Hassan Fathy was selected for the strategic mission. The site was in Luxor, some 500 km south of Cairo in a rural, arid and underdeveloped part of the country. Hassan Fathy accepted the mandate with great enthusiasm as it rhymed with his own professional inspirations and philosophies. Without delay, Hassan Fathy said good bye to Cairo and took the Upper Egypt train to Luxor heading south. In Luxor, Hassan Fathy was destined to face challenges and fight resistance, however also to make history and achieve greatness.

What Makes This Project Great

New Al Gourna village marks a turning point in the history by using Architecture to serve the poor in a sustainable and economic manner. Moreover, the following 10 points explain why the New Al Gourna is great by any measure or standard:

1. Introduced a new knowledge area termed "Architecture for the Poor."
2. Pioneered sustainable Green Building that later on became a worldwide trend.
3. Hassan Fathy is considered the best-known Egyptian Architect since the great Imhotep.
4. Provided a perfect prototype of zero energy natural cooling heat ventilation systems.
5. An example for cultural preservation and heritage continuation through architecture.
6. Revived the ancient Egyptian method of building vaults and domes using mudbricks.
7. Gained wide international recognition and respect way after its application till today.
8. Arch Hassan Fathy received the first Aga Khan Chairman's Award in 1980 AD.
9. Project has been listed with WMF and UNESCO's World Monuments Watch in 2010 AD.
10. Featured in a Google Doodle in 2017 AD as a pioneering new method in Architecture.

Story Starring and Key Characters

Figure 6.2 Hassan Fathy [2]

Table 6.1 Biography of Architect Hassan Fathy

Name	**Hassan Fathy**
Party	Independent
Title	Architect of the Poor
Legacy	An Egyptian Architect, master builder, poet, and philosopher who devoted his life to improve lifestyle of the poor through enhanced architecture. Invented the "Architecture for the Poor" blending vernacular philosophy and green building. Winner of Aga Khan's Award and his New Gourna village has become a famous world monument protected by WMF and UNESCO.
PM Role	Project Manager, Architect, and Master Builder

Hassan Fathy (Figure 6.2), 1900–1989 AD, was an Egyptian architect, university professor, master builder, poet, writer, speaker, and philosopher. Hassan Fathy was born in Alexandria/Egypt to a wealthy family of an Egyptian father and Turkish mother. He studied Architecture at King Fouad University, now Cairo University, and graduated as an Architect in 1926 AD. His first project was the design and construction of countryside public schools for Egypt's Ministry of Education. That project gave him firsthand understanding of how poor people lived and how construction was conducted in poor villages. Along his career, Hassan Fathy designed over 160 building projects ranging from modest country houses to fully planned urban developments. However, the crown diamond in Hassan Fathy's career remains the New Al Gourna village, through which he got international fame and reputation as founder of modern sustainable green building and the Architecture of the Poor. He is also widely regarded as Egypt's best-known architect since Imhotep. Hassan Fathy died in 1989 AD at the age of 89 after a long life full of achievements and a lasting impact on architecture.

6.1 Exposition: A Royal Decree to Relocate the Gourna Village

Figure 6.3 Location map of Al Gourna village, Luxor, Egypt [3]

It's the year 1946 AD. The Second World War's dust has just settled, and governments around the world are getting back to normal. Egypt has not been directly or massively hit by the war; however, many programs stopped or slowed down awaiting the war to end. One of the key pending programs for the Egyptian government at the time was the protection of ancient sites against looting and illegal trading. High on the list was the village of Al Gourna, a small village located on the west bank of the Nile River near Luxor city, 660 km south to Egypt's capital Cairo, as shown in Figure 6.3. Al Gourna village founded itself in the 1800s AD atop the Tombs of the Nobles archeological site. The village was long reported to be living on tomb raiding and selling the stolen artifacts. Finally, a royal decree was issued in 1946 AD to relocate the village away from the archaeological site to a new village to be built for them. The mandate was serious, urgent, and immediate. Meanwhile, Architect Hassan Fathy was busy building governmental village schools, and was doing great. As such, based on his excellent reputation as a talented architect and go-getter, the Egyptian Department of Antiquates decided to appoint Architect Hassan Fathy to take charge of the New Al Gourna village project. Hassan Fathy accepted the mandate with enthusiasm. He understood the mandate and was determined to change the status quo and do the job in an exemplary manner. After all, he had previous knowledge of the Nubian architecture, gained through his 1941 AD visit to Luxor, so was ready to hit the ground running. On the day of traveling from Cairo to Luxor, he headed to the Egyptian Department of Antiquities (DoA) headquarters to meet with the officials and thank them one more time for their trust. Before noon, he was in Cairo's main railway station to take the early afternoon train heading to Luxor. Twilight next day, the train arrived to Luxor railway station. The architect-on-a-national-mission spent the first night in a modest public hotel in Luxor. Dawn next morning he was on his way to Al Gourna village to meet with the villagers, introduce himself, and agree the way forward. As he approached the village, on a rough narrow road, he got stopped by three masked and armed men, who took him to the mayor of the village, or the Umdah. To Hassan Fathy's surprise, the old and wise Umdah knew about Hassan's mission, and was indeed expecting his arrival. He welcomed Hassan and promised him full support, security, and most of all the cooperation of the villagers to make his mission a success. Hassan liked what he heard, however with caution.

6.2 Rising Action: Hassan Fathy Building Mud Palaces for the Poor

The first and foremost effort in Hassan Fathy's mission was to understand the village's existing prevailing culture and urban conditions. Scenes and impressions of Al Gourna village are shown in Figures 6.4 and 6.5. His investigation covered the villager's traditions, demography, mentality, culture, habits, and socioeconomic conditions. He began with talking to people, then proceeded to studying the village's current urban planning and architecture. Findings were absolutely interesting. On the infrastructure level, the village was built illegally, so was not given access to utilities such as clean water, electricity, and sewage systems. On the socioeconomic level, community consisted of five tribes living and ca 120 families, and four district zones. The society placed high value on tribalism and privacy of families, especially women, and people were so proud of their pharaonic ancestry. Stealing and selling monuments were never revealed or admitted by residents. However, that was not part of Hassan Fathy's mandate, so he decided to focus on his core mission, which is building a new village for the folks to move to and settle in. The engineering job had two key aspects in it, namely, Urban Planning comprising district zoning and streets layout, and, House Architecture comprising space programming, architectural features, and building techniques. Above all, the job constituted bringing about a major change to the village and villagers. The following paragraphs discuss the change from existing to new conditions and in-between Hassan Fathy's philosophy of change through architecture.

Figure 6.4 Al Gourna village, Luxor, Egypt [4]

Existing Urban Planning

The village was planned by its inhabitants, with no evidence of any structured pattern. However, the random existing urban planning took account of certain key considerations such as security, community cohesion, and interdependence of the members of the society. Houses were built adjacent to each other, creating dense residential constellations separated by narrow streets leading to main streets in irregular patterns (Figure 6.5). Domestic shops and small factories were located in the basement of residential houses, especially those located on main streets. The village had a central mosque and a central water store; however, no evidence of schools or social activities. For transportation of passengers and goods, the villagers didn't rely on mechanical vehicles; instead they used donkeys, or just walked. Water was supplied directly from the nearby river using clay jars borne over heads of women. For defecation, the villagers used an open area on the outskirts of the village, primarily in the night time, however not free of embarrassment and illness.

Figure 6.5 The irregular urban planning of Old Al Gourna village [5]

Existing Houses Architecture and Construction

Most village houses were also designed and constructed by the village residents using vernacular architecture and construction to fit their own needs. Building heights ranged from one to two stories, usually starting with a ground floor, then adding a first floor to accommodate sons when they got married. The room dimensions and wall thicknesses were defined by the residents, just like in making clay pots. Vision to hands to reality. Walls were made of baked mud bricks and roofs were made of timber framework. Ironically, houses were commonly shared with pets, cows, and donkeys that were treated as members of the family. Such primitive living conditions combined with the lack of clean water or drainage resulted in the spread of diseases and reduced people's life expectations. That fact was so shocking to Hassan Fathy and enhanced his determination to do something to these people through proper architecture. On the other hand, houses were decorated with simple drawings and writings inspired by native arts and religious features so they become easily identifiable. Ironically, all in all, people seemed to be happy with their lives and attached to their village and houses. That left Hassan Fathy pondering, and indeed somewhat worried, that the new village has got to be attractive enough to convince the villagers to abandon their beloved village and follow him to the new village, the promised paradise.

Hassan Fathy's Design Philosophy

Hassan Fathy's conviction was that people naturally aspire for a better life, and that a better life can be achieved through better architecture and urban planning. Al Gourna villagers were no exception, they also dreamed of a better life, however always defeated by fear, poverty, and rejection. Hassan Fathy's mission was therefore a unique opportunity for the villagers to change their lives to the better. After all, work is funded by the government. The fear of change however remained in the villagers' hearts. If they have to move to the new village, they will also have to miss the wealth they can make by robbing tombs. They just didn't know what to say at the moment; so, buying time, and waiting to see the outcome of his work, they decided to let the government's envoy Hassan Fathy proceed with his mission. What the villagers surely realized was that Hassan Fathy came to work with them, and for them. In his book *Architecture of the Poor*, Hassan Fathy wrote: "While the characteristics of a living creature are irrevocably settled at the moment of fertilization, the characteristics of a building are determined by the whole complex of decisions made by everyone that has a say in the matter, at every stage of its construction" (Fathy, 1973). So Design and Construction were carried out in three distinct steps, namely: (1) New Village Urban Planning; (2) New Houses Planning and Design; and (3) New Village Construction.

New Village Urban Planning

At the end of his initial filed survey, Hassan Fathy was fully charged with energy and ideas. He thanked everyone and rushed back to his room and closed the door. He opened the window to the fresh air and golden sun rays, closed his eyes, had a deep breath, then turned his head, opened his eyes, and looked at his drawing board. He approached it slowly, tape fixed a new blank drawing sheet on it, and sat down thinking. The new layout has got to be a game changer, turning the stagnant patterns to dynamic, and chaos and despair to clarity and hope. The first key task was to create the new village layout, or a Master Plan, including zoning, streets, squares, blocks, and public facilities. Slowly, he pulled a pencil and touched the drawing board with a first lateral line. The Master Plan had to satisfy the needs of the villagers and the vision of the architect. The Master Planning process has three parts, namely, Inputs, Tools and Techniques, and Outputs.

First, the Inputs part included the site, the budget, the time frame, and the desired capacity and phasing. The allocated site had an area of 50 acres located a few kilometers from the old village, outside of the valley of tombs. The site was bounded by a national highway and located right outside the river flooding corridor. The budget was not fixed by authorities, however construction was expected to be low cost. The time frame was also basically as soon as possible. The targeted ultimate capacity was 900 families, with an urgent first phase of 120 families aiming to lodge the existing Al Gourna population. The extra capacity was meant to mainly accommodate future settlers from the region, as well as to take account of the expected organic expansion of the village population with time.

Secondly, the Tools and Techniques part included a range of cutting-edge urban planning concepts. In order to maintain social stability, the village was divided into four main neighborhoods to accommodate the four tribal groups of the existing village. Neighborhoods were separated by 10-m wide main streets to mark off boundary lines between neighborhoods as well as to allow for good town ventilation and movement. The in–out trip started from the individual residential houses, out to 6-m short narrow private streets where children can play, on to semiprivate squares for residents and their families, further on to 10-m wide public main streets leading to major public buildings and the village's main downtown square. The scheme was implemented using angular streets zigzagging the street users in and out to enhance privacy and enrich the pedestrians' outdoor experience. Public buildings were provided in two groups, namely, the Downtown and the Outskirts. The Downtown group was located in the heart of the village and included private facilities such as Grand Mosque, Village Hall, Community Theatre, Sporting Club, Village Crafts Exhibition, Khan Shops, Church, and a public Hammam providing public baths. On the other hand, the Outskirts group was located along the village outer borders and included such facilities that may involve people from outside the village such as the Market Place, Crafts School, Police Station, Women's Social Center, Girls Primary School, Boys Primary School, and an Artificial Lake and Park.

And, thirdly, the Outputs part of the master planning exercise, which included a well-thought-out Master Plan, as shown in Figure 6.6. A unique Master Plan that will keep architects from all over the world staring at it for generations to come. The inventive master plan was not only designed to address the villager's needs, but also to achieve Hassan Fathy's vision of improving the villagers' life style. That includes a new safe, clean, and healthy place where they can learn crafts, sell products, and make a living without having to steal tombs and be constantly threatened by law enforcement. A new life and a brighter future for the families and their children, free of fear, disease, and illiteracy.

New Houses Planning and Design

After completing the Master Plan, the next stage was to engineer and build the village houses and buildings. Still not an easy task. Design needs to be innovative yet matching residents' needs and expectations. Construction needs to be simple, strong, and low cost. The great Architect sat for

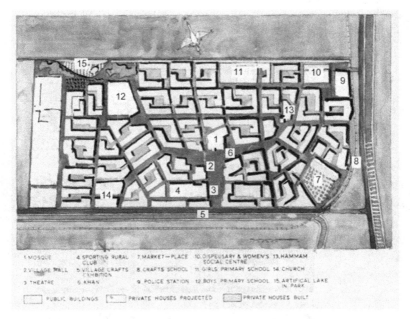

Figure 6.6 Master Plan of New Al Gourna village by
Hassan Fathy [6]

hours staring into the blue sky, recollecting his experiences, philosophies, and engineering principles. With the authority given to him by the government, he knew it's his opportunity to bring about greatness, and implement his revolutionary ideas. He daydreamed the happy end and the world applause for this spectacular success. As to Design, Hassan Fathy had three references and principles. The three effects were the Islamic architecture displayed in Old Cairo, the ancient construction method of using mud and mudbrick, and the vernacular Nubian architecture that prevailed in Upper Egypt at the time. And, the three design principles were privacy, culture preservation, and sustainability. As such, he effected several axiomatic concept improvements to the design of old houses. Old houses combined humans and animals in the same space. New houses separated animals and assigned them different entrances or different floors. Another concept change was that bedrooms should take place away from noisy rooms; therefore, houses were designed in two stories, ground floor for house activities and first floor for bedrooms. Figure 6.7 shows an example of New Al Gourna houses, namely a building block combining two attached smaller family and larger family dwelling units. Legend explains the components of the space program.

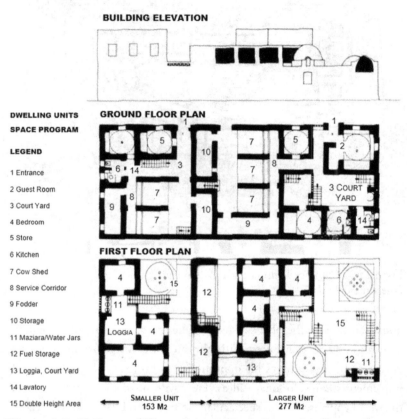

BUILDING ELEVATION

DWELLING UNITS
SPACE PROGRAM

LEGEND

1 Entrance
2 Guest Room
3 Court Yard
4 Bedroom
5 Store
6 Kitchen
7 Cow Shed
8 Service Corridor
9 Fodder
10 Storage
11 Maziara/Water Jars
12 Fuel Storage
13 Loggia, Court Yard
14 Lavatory
15 Double Height Area

GROUND FLOOR PLAN

FIRST FLOOR PLAN

SMALLER UNIT
153 M2

LARGER UNIT
277 M2

Figure 6.7 Al Gourna Village, Luxor, Egypt (Image by: Bernard Gagnon) [7]

Given the hot temperature in the area, cooling of buildings was of paramount importance in the building design. This is when Hassan Fathy first started to think green building. He introduced an effective natural cooling system with no power resource required apart from the principles of physics and ancient nature aerodynamic cooling techniques. The system simply depended on allowing air to flow through the buildings pushing hot air out. This was achieved by using a combination of two simple techniques adopted from ancient mansions in Old Cairo. The first is the use of dome roofs instead of traditional flat roofs. The spherical shape of domes enables a shaded thus cooler part of the roof most of the day. It also creates an internal concavity that collects lighter hot air and vents it out of the building through the thermodynamics phenomenon of convective ventilation. In convective ventilation, natural air movement relies on the increased buoyancy of warm air that rises to escape the building through high level outlets created in the domes. That draws in lower level cooler, causing room temperature to drop and natural cooling to happen. The second technique has to do with aerodynamics passive ventilation (PV) or the process of supplying air to and removing air from an indoor space without using mechanical systems. The combination of the two natural ventilation and cooling techniques was enabled by the use of Mashrabiya windows as shown in Figure 6.8. Mashrabiyas are window screens widely in old Cairo mansions, usually made of wood, however in New Al Gourna they were made of mud bricks. Mashrabiyas have great building cooling effects. They break the harsh sun rays and reduce temperature of the air running through them by increasing its pressure. In addition, they provide privacy since the building inside can't be seen from outside, whereas outside can be seen from inside. Besides, on the social side of the design, Hassan Fathy was amazed to explain that to the conservative villagers that, behind these Mashrabiya windows, ladies of the house may sit and comfortably watch the street in perfect privacy without the need to hide behind curtains.

New Village Construction

So at this point, Hassan Fathy's design aspirations and concepts were put on paper. He felt a big relief, took a deep breath, and started thinking about the next step, Construction. Hassan Fathy was determined to using 100 percent local materials and local resources. The local materials were basically clays and mud taken from the very agricultural fields where the new village is going to be built. Moreover, he was determined to have the villagers build their own houses, brick by brick, dome by dome. In doing that, the villagers will become totally construction wise fully independent and self-sufficient. That's a key unstated objective of Hassan Fathy's school of thought, which chiefly aim to honor the poor and to yield architecture, science, and technology to serve them and improve

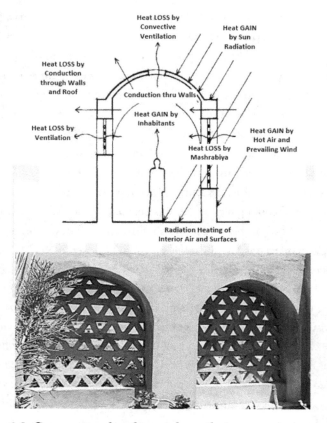

Figure 6.8 Green natural cooling and ventilation system using Mashrabiyas [8]

their lives. Naturally, the villagers required training which Hassan Fathy was happy to do, hands on. To Hassan's surprise, the villagers also had own vernacular building skills. After all, their ancestors are the ancient Egyptians who impressed the world with their unmatched building skills and eternal temples, tombs, and pyramids. Figure 6.9 shows pictures of the villagers at work building their own future, brick by brick, vault by vault. Bricks were cast in an on-site brickyard. Ideally, such a brickyard should be situated outside the area scheduled for building, so that it does not have to be moved when its site is needed (Fathy 1973).

Another key challenge was providing the village with proper water supply and wastewater drainage systems. As to water, and instead of getting it from the river muddy and contaminated, neighborhoods were

Figure 6.9 Al Gournis training and then building their own new village [9]

provided with deep wells operated with hand pumps drawing water from deep down free from harmful bacteria. As to drainage, and instead of the dreadful public defecation yards, gravity drains were provided to collect foul sewer from houses and lead it to common septic tanks shared between rows of houses or about 10 families. The objective of the first construction stage of the New Al Gourna village was to build enough number of residential buildings and units to accommodate the existing families, residents of the Old Al Gourna village, in addition to a range of key public buildings such as the Mosque, the Shops, the Schools, and the Market Place. The rest of the Master Plan buildings and houses were planned to be built gradually over time as the community grows and the demand increases. Step by step, building by building, the design training, manufacturing, and construction processes of the first stage of the new village moved forward orchestrated by Hassan Fathy. The new village design introduced a wide range of deliberate design changes and functional enhancements, which aimed to improve the life of the villagers. Since building works had to be limited to times of the river flooding yearly season when farmers had to stop working in fields, it took construction three seasons to deliver first benefits and buildings. A study conducted by the Ministry of Social Affairs revealed that the mudbrick-based method of Hassan Fathy can indeed reduce building cost to half when compared with concrete-based construction. That was a major tick box and a key success indicator. So finally, the first construction phase of the New Al Gourna village was substantially completed, fully functional, and ready to receive its residents. As such, the time has come for the Gournis to bid farewell to their old village and move to the new village, the promised paradise. And that's when a major drama was about to happen. The photo in Figure 6.10 is of high symbolism. The young village girl riding the donkey away is throwing a final look at her old village, whereas the donkey is still heading back.

Figure 6.10 A village girl bidding farewell to her old Al Gourna home [10]

6.3 Climax: Project Completion and Celebration

In 1949 AD, Hassan Fathy, notified the Department of Antiquities of the first phase completion. The new village looked like a beautiful camel embodying the magic and magic of ancient Egyptian architecture. The universe loved the new village, and the nature celebrated the birth of green architecture. As shown in Figures 6.11 and 6.12, the self-colored yellow-brownish mud buildings stood proud beautifully contrasting with the color of the blue sky, then turned into mud palaces. Hassan Fathy was so proud of his dream-come-true village, so stood staring at its walls and domes, and at the happy faces of the people around him. The village's innovative characteristics proved Hassan Fathy's idea that, with the use of local materials and legacy techniques, sustainable human development and social cohesion can be achieved with vernacular architecture. However, to Hassan Fathy's surprise, the Gournis were much less excited about their meant-to-be new home and attractive mud palaces. In fact their leadership rejected the project and refused to move in to their new dedicated houses. That's despite Hassan Fathy's serious attempts to secure the Gournis' buy in and to engage them during design and construction. The primary reason for rejection declared by the Gournis was the excessive use of domes, which made the village look like a graveyard. In the Gournis' culture and minds, domes are for the dead and indicate having graves below them. Gourna women, however, were slightly receptive of the village and the new houses for their wide spaces, respect of privacy, and attractive interior design. Gourna men, to the contrary, were bluntly against the idea and insisted not to relocate. Men won the battle and families did not relocate except a very few. Hassan Fathy attempted to soften the Gournis' stance by taking them on tours in and around the village and the buildings, however in vain. Hassan Fathy flew back to Cairo to report the state of affairs to the Department of Antiquities, only to receive little sympathy or consideration. Project slowed down and the decision on how to proceed was put in the hands of the Department of Antiquities.

Figure 6.11 New Al Gourna—Downtown [11]

Figure 6.12 New Al Gourna—Grand Mosque [12]

6.4 Falling Action: Village Gets Criticized and Abandoned

News about Hassan Fathy's failure caused by the rejection of the villagers to relocate to the new village became the talk-of-the-town in Cairo and across the country. Critics echoed that the domed architecture Hassan Fathy championed was indeed an architectural blunder given that, traditionally, domes were used for funerary architecture rather than residential spaces. Hassan Fathy didn't agree with that vision and referred the reluctance to move to a hidden agenda of the tomb robbers. Others questioned the wide application of mudbrick construction for stability and durability concerns, also as a step that goes against the winds of modernization, which prevailed at the time. Hassan Fathy rejected such claims citing the fact that mudbrick construction is very well established in the country, and that modernization does not mean abandoning own heritage and adopting western model and architectural style. Leftist didn't miss the opportunity to accuse Hassan Fathy of being just another elite of western mentality and education who is trying to impose his romantic views on the poor from a high point. Hassan Fathy didn't quite respond to such allegations. Instead, he just kept stressing that his objective was to make it possible for the poor to have gracious and healthy housing facilities at a low cost and built in an environmentally friendly manner using strictly local materials and resources. In Cairo, politicians began to wonder why this was happening and some suggested the use of law enforcement to implement the relocation of the villagers involved in the trade of antiquities stolen from the royal necropolis. However, despite local criticism and charges, Hassan Fathy's work remained respected by all as a daring innovation of a noble cause. He remained involved with the New Al Gourna village project for a few years to complete some enhancement works and convince some more Gourna families to move to and enjoy their new houses and new village, as shown in Figure 6.13, however still with little success.

Figure 6.13 The inner courtyard in a house in New Al Gourna [13]

In 1953 AD, the passionate Architect got exhausted with the case and decided to return to Cairo. Unfortunately, after six years of creative work, due to lack of government backing, the scheme was abandoned and left in the hands of the villagers and local intruders from all walks of life. Hassan Fathy began his new life in Cairo heading the Architectural Section of the Faculty of Fine Arts. In 1957 AD, he moved to Athens to collaborate with international planners to advocate traditional natural-energy solutions including the "Cities of the Future" research program in Africa. In 1963 AD, he returned to Cairo where he lived and worked for the rest of his life doing public speaking and private consulting around the world. In 1968, he authored a book on the New Al Gourna project, published at a limited scale by Cairo's Ministry of Culture titled *A Tale of Two Villages*, a book that was later in 1973 AD republished at large scale by the University of Chicago in the United States under its iconic name *Architecture for the Poor: An Experiment in Rural Egypt*. In 1980 AD, at the age of 80 years, Hassan Fathy crowned his career full of prizes and recognition with receiving the world renowned Aga Khan Award for Architecture's first Chairman Award in acknowledgment of his lifelong commitment to architecture in the Muslim world. In 1989 AD, Hassan Fathy died at the age of 89 years leaving behind a wealth of knowledge, philosophy, and a whole layer of architects and followers who still are inspired by his ideas and his architecture decades after his departure.

6.5 Resolution: Conservation by WMF and UNESCO

Today, many decades after its construction, much of the village buildings and architecture have been lost. Only a small portion survived and yet in a critical condition. The site has been mostly abandoned despite the educational and experimental value of the scheme, and the knowledge and philosophies embedded therein. Authorities turned a blind eye on the matter for many decades, allowing trespassing and substandard housing construction to take place in the new village's site in a catastrophic fashion, as shown in Figure 6.14. However, Hassan Fathy, and his school of "Architecture for the Poor" embodied in New Al Gourna village project, continued to inspire architects and attract world attention in the academic, architectural, sustainability, and heritage sites preservation fields. The World Monuments Fund, a New York-based nonprofit organization dedicated to preserving and protecting endangered ancient and historic sites around the world, had placed New Al Gourna the World Monuments Watch List. UNESCO and World Monuments Fund joined forces to survey the village's buildings and document conservation needs. UNESCO, in cooperation with the Egyptian Ministry of Culture and the Governorate of Luxor, also worked to preserve this precious heritage situated within the World Heritage property of ancient Egypt. In 2017 AD, Google celebrated Hassan Fathy's 117th birthday with a Google Doodle highlighting his character and green vernacular architecture including New Al Gourna village.

The story of what could be called "Al Gourna Syndrome" has been subject to numerous discussions, articles, books, papers, and research theses. However, the following words wrote by Hassan Fathy himself, remain the conclusion and wisdom of the story carrying the same genes and genuineness of the architecture of the village itself:

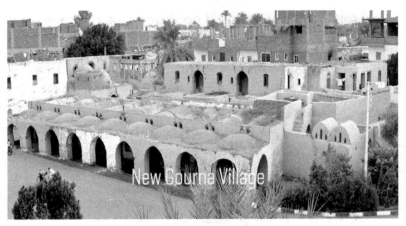

Figure 6.14 New Al Gourna ultimately encircled by ugly concrete buildings [14]

Culture springs from the roots; Seeping through all the shoots; To leaf and flower and bud; From cell to cell, like green blood; Is released by rain showers; As fragrance from the wet flowers; To fill the air! ... But, culture that is poured on men; From up above, congeals then; Like damp sugar, so they become; Like sugar-dolls, and when some; Life-giving shower wets them through; They disappear and melt into; A sticky mess! (Fathy 1973)

Story Recap Illustrated on Story Plot Diagram

The following Figure 6.15 provides overview and recap of the story spread along the five components of the typical story telling plot diagram, namely, Exposition, Rising Action, Climax, Falling Action, and Resolution.

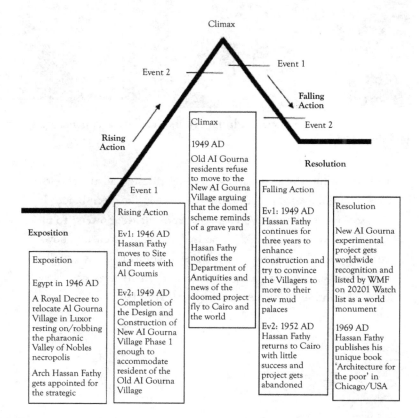

Figure 6.15 The New Al Gourna village story on story plot diagram

The Brooklyn Bridge, New York, USA—The John Roebling Family and the Story of Bridging the River to the American Dream

It's 1867 AD in New York City, New York, USA.

Immigrants pouring into New York City, mostly working in Manhattan, and living in Brooklyn. The two cities are growing fast; however, growth is restrained by the body of water separating them, the East River. New York State steps in and appoints John A. Roebling to bridge the river to the American Dream.

Figure 7.1 Brooklyn Bridge—New York, USA [1]

Table of Contents

Preface

Growth and prosperity can happen fast within a short window of opportunity. This is the story of Brooklyn Bridge shown in Figure 7.1. The enabler that played a key role in boosting New York City's economic growth by linking Brooklyn and Manhattan across the East River. The idea of linking the two cities first came up in the early 1800s AD. However, nobody knew exactly how to do that. Flying over the East River with a bridge seemed an impossible feat. Undercrossing the deep strait with a tunnel was another option, however, deemed way too costly and not free of major technical challenges. So despair prevailed, until 1831 AD with the arrival of the German immigrant John A. Roebling. John brought along special knowledge on the use of steel wire ropes in building large span suspension bridges. In 1845 AD, he started building suspension bridges using wire ropes. In 1851 AD, he built his first major 251 m (825 ft) bridge span over the Niagara River. In 1861 AD, he took the game another step further through the 322 m (1,057 ft) bridge span across the Cincinnati–Covington River. And that is when John A. Roebling got the chance to enter history by crossing the 600 m (ca 2,000 ft) wide East River, earlier thought by others to be impossible.

What Makes This Project Great

Brooklyn Bridge marks a turning point in the history of construction and engineering of large span bridges and represents the glory of the American dream. Moreover, the following 10 points explain why the Brooklyn Bridge is great by any measure or standard:

1. The world's longest bridge at the time achieving a world record status.
2. The first steel and wire ropes span suspension bridges invented by John A. Roebling.
3. The first bridge to apply the pneumatic caisson method in foundation construction.
4. The first notable women leadership in construction through Emily Warren Roebling.
5. It pioneered remote construction management through Washington and Emily Roebling.
6. It made New York City the most important commercial metropolis in the United States.
7. Marked the revival of Master Builders after centuries of design and construction split.
8. Marked the inception of the modern Design–Build project delivery approach.
9. Imposed itself as worldwide landmark attracting attention of people all over the world.
10. Designated as a NYC landmark and a National Historic Civil Engineering Landmark.

Story Starring and Key Characters

Table 7.1 Story starring and key characters

John Augustus Roebling [2]		
	Name	John Augustus Roebling
	Party	New York and Brooklyn Bridge Company
	Title	Master Builder of Bridges and Civil Engineer
	Legacy	A German immigrant civil engineer best known for designing Brooklyn Bridge in NYC. Invented the use of wire ropes in building suspension bridges that aided super large bridge spans worldwide.
	PM Role	Project Manager, Design
Washington J A Roebling [3]		
	Name	Washington J. A. Roebling
	Party	New York and Brooklyn Bridge Company
	Title	Chief Engineer of Bridge Construction
	Legacy	An American civil engineer best known for carrying on and supervising the construction of Brooklyn Bridge after the death of his father J. A. Roebling who initially designed the bridge.
	PM Role	Project Manager, Construction
Emily Warren Roebling [4]		
	Name	Emily Warren Roebling
	Party	New York and Brooklyn Bridge Company
	Title	Deputy Chief Engineer of Bridge Construction
	Legacy	An American engineer best known for her significant contribution to the completion of Brooklyn Bridge in support of her husband Washington Roebling who got seriously ill.
	PM Role	Deputy Project Manager, Construction

John Augustus Roebling, 1806–1869 AD, is a German-born American civil engineer, best known for his design of the Brooklyn Bridge. John was a master builder, bridge designer, entrepreneur, and the world pioneer of using steel wire ropes in large-span suspension bridges. In 1824 AD, he graduated from the Bauakademie in Berlin. In 1831 AD, he left Germany for the United States looking for a better future as a civil engineer. At the time, railroad cars were pulled using hemp ropes. John Roebling questioned the status quo and proposed the use of the much stronger steel wire ropes he learned about back in Germany. In 1841 AD, he began producing seven-strand wire ropes at his own factory in Saxonburg to use in railroads, and started to think about using them in suspension bridges. In 1845 AD, he began delivering several wire rope suspension bridges of increasing free spans. In April 1867 AD, he was commissioned by New York Bridge Company to design and build the Brooklyn Bridge. In 1869 AD, he completed the bridge design, however, also passed away at the age of 63 following an accident while inspecting the site before construction.

Washington John A Roebling, 1837–1926 AD, is an American civil engineer, best known for managing the construction of the Brooklyn Bridge designed by his father John A. Roebling. In 1857 AD, he graduated from the Rensselaer Polytechnic Institute in Troy, New York, specializing in suspension aqueducts. After graduation, he worked closely with his father on several suspension bridge projects. In 1867 AD, he traveled to Europe to study the latest technology in wire fabrication mills and the construction of caisson foundations (note: caissons will later bring a tragedy to Washington's life). In 1868 AD, upon his return from Germany, he joined the Brooklyn Bridge project. In 1869 AD, upon the death of John A. Roebling, he took over as the project's chief engineer. In 1872 AD, he contracted decompression sickness while working on the bridge's compressed air caisson foundations, so got incapacitated and was no longer able to leave his home. However, he continued his chief engineer duties and completed the project assisted by his wife Emily. In 1926 AD, Washington A. Roebling died at the age of 89 leaving behind his construction of the Brooklyn Bridge as a remarkable eternal legacy.

Emily Warren Roebling, 1843–1903 AD, is an American engineer best known for her significant contribution to the completion of the construction of Brooklyn Bridge. Emily deputized her husband Washington Roebling, the project's chief engineer, when he got ill and paralyzed, relaying his instructions to the site, and reporting back construction issues and progress. Emily's role was instrumental in ensuring continuation of project governance integrity, control of site operations, and driving progress until the project's safe and successful completion. In 1882 AD, when the Washington's Chief Engineer title got at risk because of his sickness, Emily faced off with New York Bridge Company, NYC authorities, engineers, and politicians and managed to save her husband's title. In 1883 AD, when the Brooklyn Bridge was completed, Emily was the first person to cross the bridge carrying a rooster as a sign of victory. In 1903 AD, Emily Warren Roebling died at the young age of 60 to stomach cancer leaving behind a great legacy of delivering the Brooklyn Bridge, superior human qualities of love, sacrifice, and matrimonial loyalty, in addition to pioneering the women's construction leadership both worldwide and historywide.

7.1 Exposition: Pressing Need to Connect Manhattan and Brooklyn

It's NYC in the 1860s AD. The U.S. economy is drifting away from agriculture toward manufacturing and industrialization. New York City places itself in the center of the action with nearly half of all U.S. exports set to pass through the New York harbor. The prospects for the country's future are fairly clear. New York City is booming. The value of lands and buildings on Manhattan is on a steep rise. Immigrants from all over the world are flowing into NYC in millions. The city and its suburbs, mainly Brooklyn, are boiling in action and delight. People live in Brooklyn and work in Manhattan across the East River. Thousands of ferries are crossing the river back and forth every day. The rhythm of life is getting faster by the day. There came the need and idea to bridge the river and close the gap. Ferry boats aren't good enough or fast enough anymore. They just don't rhyme with the new fast rhythm and upbeat of the new life in the vivid NYC exploding in enthusiasm and energy. That revived the old dream of building a bridge between the two cities and crossing the East River. But how to do that? The river is a mile wide and waters are deep and aggressive. The mission seemed to be an impossible feat, and bridge engineers everywhere confirmed the same. That was when John A. Roebling came into the picture, challenging such judgment, and vowing to cross the East River. After all, he got the secret code, his mastery and novelty of the wire rope suspension bridges. The largest bridge John A. Roebling did that far was the Cincinnati–Covington Bridge, spanning Ohio River between Cincinnati/Ohio, and Covington/Kentucky. When opened in 1866 AD, it was the longest suspension bridge in the world at 322 m (1,057 ft) main span. The new Manhattan–Brooklyn Bridge, spanning the East River, needed to be at least 50 percent larger than that. A daring technological breakthrough. But the Master Builder John A. Roebling knew what he was talking about. He understood the vast potential inherent in the wire ropes suspension bridge construction method. Greatness in construction reflected on the surface of the East River, and a historic landmark innovation was about to happen. John's confidence transferred to the leadership, which realized the window of opportunity available to make history. In February 1867 AD, the New York State's Senate passed a decree that allowed the construction of a suspension bridge from Brooklyn to Manhattan (NYT, 2018). In April 1867 AD, the New York and Brooklyn Bridge Company was established to deliver the strategic bridge, and John A. Roebling was appointed as the project's main engineer. An initial sum of USD 5 million was allocated in capital stock to fund the construction of the bridge. This sum was later supported by further USD 10 million. Figure 7.2 shows an 1860s AD aerial view and the proposed location of the planned Manhattan–Brooklyn Bridge.

7.2 Rising Action: The Roeblings Step in With a Daring Breakthrough

In April 1867 AD, John Roebling proceeded with the bridge design. The responsibility is huge, however John knew the job inside out. In, September 1867 AD, John Roebling presented the bridge's master plan (NYT, 2019). The bridge will be higher and longer than any other bridge in the world. A major civil engineering breakthrough. A do or die mission. A colossal suspension bridge with two giant offshore stone towers. As shown in Figure 7.3, the design utilized a hybrid cable-stayed/suspension

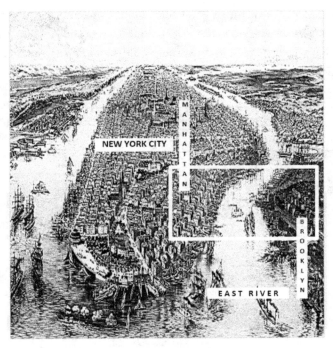

Figure 7.2 Proposed location of Brooklyn Bridge in an aerial view of NYC in the 1860s AD [5]

style. Steel truss girders for the bridge deck, and a cable anchorage block on each side of the bridge. As always, with innovation comes risk. Accurate structural analysis to assess wind and earthquake stresses was not available at the time. John Roebling response strategy was to embed high safety factors in sizing out bridge components. The strategy proved successful and the bridge lived long after construction. At this moment, all looked good and fine; however, fate was hiding a tragedy. On June 28, 1869 AD, John Roebling had a deadly accident on site. While standing at the Fulton Ferry area in Brooklyn checking the project location, his foot got crushed by an arriving ferry and his toes were severed. He caught tetanus, which caused his death in a few weeks. On July 22, 1869 AD, John Roebling passed away. Image of John Roebling can still be seen reflected in the waters of the East River. Glory to the martyrs of construction greatness. Upon John's departure, his well-trained son Washington took over and declared the project's chief engineer. Washington began by reviewing the bridge design completed by his father and developing a work breakdown structure. That included four consecutive areas of work, namely: (1) Caisson Foundations; (2) Stone Towers and Anchorages; (3) Main Suspension Cables; (4) Suspender Cables and Superstructure. Each component constituted a story of construction greatness.

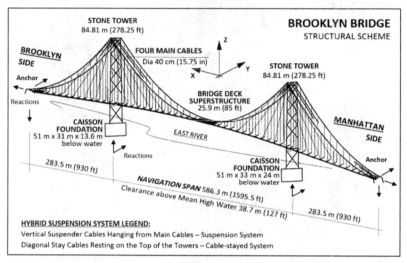

Figure 7.3 Overview of the Brooklyn Bridge hybrid structural scheme [6]

Caisson Foundations

On January 2, 1870 AD, the construction started. The first major challenge was installing the foundations of the bridge piers. Foundations had to be deep enough to reach a suitable bedrock founding level. At this point, Washington Roebling was just back from Europe where he studied the ground-breaking pneumatic caisson technology for offshore bridge foundations. Daring to innovate, the young engineer decided to use the pneumatic caissons. With innovation, however, came risks as seen later in the story. The pneumatic caisson method involves the construction of a wooden box of the size of the foundation, floating the same to the pier location, sinking the caisson into water by filling the buoyancy chambers along its boundaries with large boulders, until the caisson touches the river bed. Caisson tip edges would have iron-cutting shoes. The sinking then happens by gravity and removing the river bed soil underneath the cutting shoes, gradually until the founding level is reached. As shown in Figure 7.4, digging is carried out by labors working within air-compressed chambers. Air compression keeps chambers dry by pushing out water. Workers would climb ladders in pressure-transition shafts to get in and out of work chambers. A rapid change in pressure can cause the then new fatal caisson disease. The foundations construction progressed steadily and completed successfully in July 1872 AD. The pneumatic caisson method succeeded; however, many workers caught the caisson disease, of which several lost their lives. Glory to the martyrs of construction greatness. Ironically, a victim of the method was Washington Roebling himself who caught the caisson disease while going out of the air-compressed chambers faster than the safe speed. Washington got seriously ill and had to spend the rest of the project working from home, and the rest of his life suffering severe pain. His great wife Emily Warren Roebling stepped in to help out her husband to manage the project despite his illness. Glory to Washington and Emily who devoted their lives to achieve construction greatness.

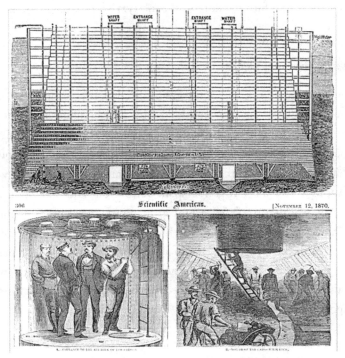

Figure 7.4 Pneumatic caisson scheme of Brooklyn Bridge [7, 8]

Stone Towers and Anchorages

In August 1872 AD, the installation of the stone towers and anchorages started. Emily took over construction management and played a key role liaising between Washington and the site teams and operations. The giant bridge towers were designed to be ca 85 m (278 ft) high with a footprint of ca 43 by 18 m (140 by 59 ft) at the water line. Towers support the four main suspension cables and the diagonal cable stays carrying the bridge deck. As shown in Figure 7.5, the stone towers had gothic style with two double-pointed arch openings, through which the roadways run. Towers were constructed using limestone and granite stone blocks bound together using adhesive cementitious material. Alongside, the anchorage blocks were constructed in parallel. Construction of the bridge towers and anchorages took about four years to complete, ending in July 1876 AD. Again, working on the giant bridge towers involved dangerous work-at-height. Many workers died during construction. Most of them were new immigrants who came to America with a big smile and hope for a bright future. Glory to the martyrs of construction greatness.

Main Suspension Cables

In August 1876 AD, the construction of the suspension main cables started. This operation was considered by bridge engineers at the time to be an impossible feat. The massive 16 in (40 cm) diameter cables had to begin at one anchorage block on one side of the river, take off and fly high to touch upon the top of the first giant tower, sag down within the super wide main navigation span, bottom out and take off again to touch upon the top of the second giant tower, then end their journey leaning down toward and anchored into the other anchorage block on the other side of the East River. The incredible operation was made possible using a special cable extension apparatus invented by John Roebling. To test the system, two wires were stretched between the towers to create a temporary footbridge for workers. As shown in Figure 7.6, the first wire

Figure 7.5 The Brooklyn Bridge limestone suspension tower [9]

was tested by sending across an engineer in a chair traveler hung from the wire. A thrilling scene witnessed by a crowd of 10,000 people. Emily was watching the scene with thrill on her face and tears in her eyes in fear for the man and appreciation of the historic moment. Glory to the brave engineer Edmund Fisher Farrington who risked his life for the sake of construction greatness.

Figure 7.6 E. F. Farrington zip lining the East River on a wire traveler [10]

As shown in Figure 7.7, the temporary walkway was operated under strict safety conditions such as limiting the number of users to 25 men at any time. This early achievement boosted team motivation and spirits. The heavy work followed, spinning wires and installing the four principal load carrying cables responsible for carrying bridge deck loads from the deck to the towers across the bridge spans. Wire after wire, spinning wheels spun the four main suspension cables across the mile from shore to shore. Work had to be performed continuously and precisely to ensure cables strength and alignment. All four cables had a parabolic vertical profile, and the two middle cables had to be shifted laterally outward to make way for the bridge deck central promenade.

By May 1878 AD, when installation of the four main cables was past midway, one of the wires slipped, injuring three workers, and killing two

Figure 7.7 Walkway, traveler wheel, and suspension cable system ready to start [11]

others. Glory to the martyrs of construction greatness. Later on, a major cable procurement outrage was announced. It was discovered that a wires' supplier, who was appointed by the owner's trustees despite Washington's preservation, had deceivingly provided inferior quality wires. Of 80 wire rings tested on site, only 5 passed. It was too late and too difficult to replace the suspected cables. Chief Engineer Washington looked into the matter and determined that the cables are acceptable as built, and that bridge is still four times as strong as necessary, instead of six to eight times as originally designed by John Roebling. However, in order to maintain the same level of safety, 150 additional wires were added to each cable at the wire supplier's expense, and life went on. By October 1878 AD, the last of the main cables wires was spun marking completion of the main cables installation.

Suspender Cables and Superstructure

In March 1879 AD, the construction of the suspender cables and bridge was ready to start. Suspender cables and superstructure works constituted installing the vertical suspenders, the diagonal cable stays, along with the six 10-m (33 ft) longitudinal steel truss girders, and the steel cross beams, forming together the bridge's superstructure supporting the roadway. Steel trusses were held up by suspender ropes hanging from the four main cables, and the cable stays resting on the top of the two bridge towers. Steel crossbeams ran across the longitudinal trusses, along with a range of stiffener beams to tie the bridge deck elements together. Unfortunately, the site was ready to start; however, there was a delay by the owner in the supply of structural steel works due to cash issues. As a mitigation, a small quantity of 1,000 short tons (900 long tons) steel trusses was purchased to keep things going on site until the bulk of steel elements is procured. Throughout the delays, Washington and Emily presented the mayors of New York and Brooklyn with a monthly construction progress report. The project, however, was in constant delay and slow rate of progress due to trustees' negative involvement and steel procurement issues. New York and Brooklyn Company board of trustees got increasingly dismayed, and instead of speaking with the trustees, they wanted to replace Washington Roebling. Emily the great got into the picture and defended her husband, passionately, logically, and successfully.

On the other hand, opposition from shipbuilders began to surface claiming that the bridge would not provide sufficient clearance underneath for their ships, as well as from civil engineers who suspected the bridge's structural adequacy. After deliberation, however, the Supreme Court decided that the Brooklyn Bridge was indeed a legitimate structure. The construction of the Brooklyn Bridge took ca 14 years' time and 15 million USD to complete. In 1883 AD, bridge construction was completed, marking a great civil engineering achievement. It pushed the technologies of the time to new limits, and added to the world a remarkable piece of sophisticated construction. The design and construction of Brooklyn Bridge was chiefly the make of first and second generations of immigrants, working under the U.S. flag. Glory to the engineers, workers, and martyrs of construction greatness.

7.3 Climax: Project Completion and Celebration

On May 24, 1883 AD, the then called "New York and Brooklyn Bridge" was officially opened to the public in a splendid popular celebration. The giant bridge looked so thrilling on the day that it was almost worshiped by viewers. The longest free span suspension bridge in the world. New York City and Brooklyn are now connected by a bridge for pedestrians, horse-drawn carriages, cable cars, and elevated railroads. The dream came true. The celebration was witnessed by thousands of happy folks over the bridge, and happy ships below the bridge in the East River. Cheering, flags, banners, fireworks, and gunfire. The East River, itself, was watching the action and wondering what's going on. It soon realized that the first bridge to cross the river became a reality, and that many several bridge invasions might follow in the future. John Roebling didn't live long to witness that day; however, his soul could be seen in the sky above the bridge, watching the day with a big smile, proud of Washington and Emily and their team. The audience was cheering in joy, and Emily was in a different world hiding her tears and remembering all what she and the Roeblings went through in the past 14 years since the project began. The official opening of the highly strategic bridge was attended by the 21st president of the United States, President Chester Alan Arthur. Figure 7.8 shows a newspaper announcement of Brooklyn Bridge opening. New York Mayor Franklin Edson crossed the bridge and shook hands with Brooklyn Mayor Seth Low on the promenade in a highly symbolic gesture. The ceremony's principal address was given by trustee Abram Stevens Hewitt whose words were crafted to be remembered and to reflect the true spirit and worth of the great project. He said, speaking about the bridge: "It is not the work of any one man or of any one age. It is the result of the study, of the experience, and of the knowledge of many men in many ages. It is not merely a creation; it is a growth. It stands before us today as the sum and epitome of human knowledge; as the very heir of the ages; as the latest glory of centuries of patient observation, profound study and accumulated skill, gained, step by step, in the never-ending struggle of man to subdue the forces of nature to his control and use" (Chisholm, 1911). In the early period of operation, the bridge served ca 2,000 vehicles and 150,000 people a day in several transit ways and modes. Figure 7.9 shows an overview of Brooklyn Bridge. Figure 7.10 shows a depiction of a cross section of the bridge's transport modes and functions. The mass transit system, however, was not commissioned on the day of the opening and was operated at a later time. As the New York and Brooklyn Bridge was the only bridge across the East River at that time, it was also first called the East River Bridge. Impressed by the greatness of the giant bridge, it was hailed by the media as the eighth wonder of the world. The new bridge also had a great commercial and strategic significance. It changed the face of life and economy in the entire region and put New York City on the path to become the most important commercial hub and cultural metropolis in the United States of America and the world.

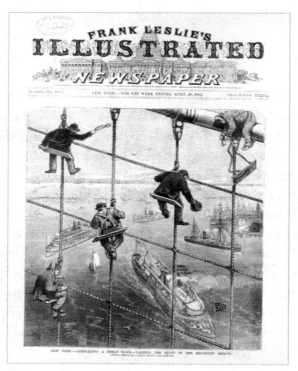

Figure 7.8 Newspaper announcement of Brooklyn Bridge opening [12]

Figure 7.9 Official popular celebration of the Brooklyn Bridge opening [13]

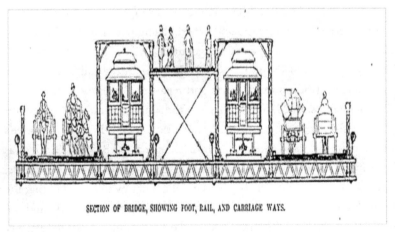

Figure 7.10 Cross section of bridge's transport modes and functions [14]

7.4 Falling Action: Brooklyn Bridge and the Test of Time

Immediately following the Brooklyn Bridge opening in 1883 AD, New York City started to see a major industrial boom and a socioeconomic transformation. The new function of uninterrupted land transportation between Manhattan and Brooklyn, enabled by the new bridge, encouraged many people to settle in Brooklyn and work in Manhattan. In less than 15 years after bridge opening, Brooklyn's population almost doubled to reach one million inhabitants. Over the years, the two independent cities merged into one. In 1898 AD, Brooklyn got unified with New York City, and the Brooklyn Bridge came under the stewardship of the new greater NYC. On the bridge integrity and passing the test of time, the first concerns about bridge strength were raised in 1898 AD. A traffic backup due to a dead horse caused one of the truss cords to buckle. Shortly thereafter, in 1901 AD, more serious concerns were raised after 12 suspender cables snapped. There came the idea, and indeed the need to construct more bridges across the East River to relieve the traffic pressure off the aging sole bridge. In 1905 AD, the Brooklyn Transit Company confirmed that the bridge had reached its load-carrying capacity. In 1915 AD, the East River Bridge was officially renamed to its current name "Brooklyn Bridge." In 1922 AD, two bridge cables were reported to have slipped, resulting in banning motor vehicles from using the Brooklyn Bridge. Figure 7.11 shows an overview of the bridge in 1933 AD. In 1948 AD, a first major renovation of the Brooklyn Bridge was carried out in 1954 AD. Several renovation and maintenance efforts were and are still being performed by New York City to keep the iconic ancient bridge intact. In 2016 AD, the New York City Department of Transport (NYCDOT) announced a plan to reinforce the Brooklyn Bridge's foundations and repair the masonry arches on the approach ramps. In 2018 AD, the New York City Landmarks Preservation Commission approved a further renovation of the Brooklyn Bridge's suspension towers and approach ramps. So, in fact, the Brooklyn Bridge has been living on innovations and retrofitting works for quite some time. The ancient stone and steel bridge is getting older by the day, fighting the inevitable natural aging, and resisting the harsh weather of NYC and the marine conditions of the East River. Without a doubt, the East River never liked the Brooklyn Bridge; however, the innocent bridge only wanted to serve the people of Manhattan and Brooklyn. Apologies to the East River, and glory to the Brooklyn Bridge's caretakers who strive every day to keep the ancient civil engineering icon happy, alive and in good health, serving

Figure 7.11 Overview of Brooklyn Bridge from Brooklyn showing Manhattan 1933 AD [15]

people and inspiring architects, engineers, artists, and even lovers all over the world.

7.5 Resolution: The Brooklyn Bridge Today

Today, the Brooklyn Bridge is a key iconic structure on the world stage. It forms a unique and highly recognizable feature on the world's and the history's construction skyline. It keeps engineers and architects pondering how it was planned, designed, and built. Brooklyn Bridge simply symbolizes the American dream in terms of opportunity, freedom, and industrialization. It opened the door for all suspension bridges that we see today all over the world. It won numerous professional awards and appeared in endless number of magazines, movies, and songs. In 1964 AD, Brooklyn Bridge was listed as a U.S. National Historic Landmark. In 1966 AD, the bridge was added to the National Register of Historic Places. In 1972 AD, the bridge was named a National Historic Civil Engineering Landmark. And recently, in 2017 AD, it was placed on UNESCO's list of World Heritage Sites. It earned its status. Figure 7.12 shows a recent photo of the bridge promenade, tower, and cables. The Brooklyn Bridge also became an inspiring world touristic attraction point. I am proud to be a big fan and lover of the Brooklyn Bridge. I remember my first visit to NYC back in 2008 AD. I was in the United States for a PMI project management conference in Denver, Colorado. Finished the conference and decided to "Fly to New York City." Spent the night in New Jersey at a Holiday Inn, dreaming of the morning in NYC at the Brooklyn Bridge. In the morning, my old friend and classmate picked me up at the hotel with his old tiny Volkswagen, which happened to be a convertible. On the way to Brooklyn Bridge, I was counting the seconds to lay my eyes on the Brooklyn Bridge. When my brain first recorded the bridge image, I found myself yelling, OMG! It's Brooklyn Bridge! John Augustus Roebling! My friend was astonished by my reaction. In reality, the ancient steel and stone bridge looked so charming. Just like a warm mature lady, with the years only giving her more charm and beauty. When on the bridge, the suspension cables gave me the feeling of being on a swing hanging to the sky. We crossed the bridge from Manhattan side toward Brooklyn, then back to find a place to pose and take some pictures. Figure 7.13 shows me, the author of this book, posing with the Brooklyn Bridge in the background. At night, when you cross the bridge, you get the feeling you were back home, right in the narrow streets of your old town. Several bronze plaques are posted at the bridge entrance and anchorage. Of which I liked most, the one posted by The Brooklyn Engineers Club in 1951 AD. The reason is that it mentioned the great Emily Warren Roebling. The plaque reads: "The Builders of the Bridge; Dedicated to the Memory of: Emily Warren Roebling; 1843–1903; whose faith and courage helped her stricken husband; Col. Washington A. Roebling C.E.; 1837–1926; complete the construction of this bridge; from the plans of his father; John A. Roebling C.E.; 1805–1869; who gave his life to the bridge; back of every great work we can find; 'the self-sacrificing devotion of a woman'; this tablet erected 1951 by; The Brooklyn Engineers Club; with funds raised by popular subscription." The only thing that I really wished the plaques would have also mentioned is the great unknown workers, the people the heroes who spent or even lost their lives by

Figure 7.12 A recent view of the Brooklyn Bridge central pedestrian promenade [16]

Figure 7.13 Author with Brooklyn Bridge in the background, 2008 AD

participating in the construction of the Brooklyn Bridge. Glory to the Brooklyn Bridge's great engineers and workers, the heroes and martyrs of construction greatness and their families.

Story Recap Illustrated on Story Plot Diagram

The following Figure 7.14 provides overview and recap of the story spread along the five components of the typical story telling plot diagram, namely, Exposition, Rising Action, Climax, Falling Action, and Resolution.

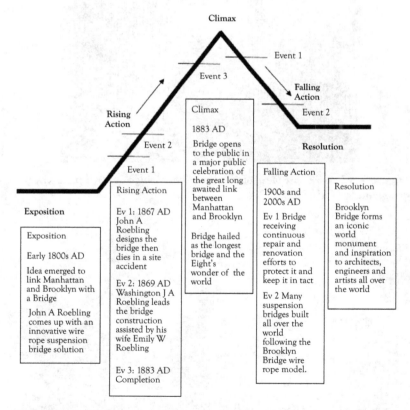

Figure 7.14 The Brooklyn Bridge story on story plot diagram

CHAPTER 8

The Crystal Palace, London, UK—Sir Joseph Paxton and the Royal Ghost That Appeared Twice Before Vanishing in the Flames

It's 1850 AD in London, England, UK.

The world is having a new beginning after the first Industrial Revolution. A new world of gears and machines. The British Queen invites the world to celebrate the glorious moment. The celebration had to be great, the moment had to glitter, and modernity had to show. That's when the sparkling Crystal Palace shined on the horizon.

Figure 8.1 The Crystal Palace, London, UK [1]

Table of Contents

Preface

The greatest legacy one can leave behind after passing away is a great story. Footprints on the sands of time for future generations to follow. This goes for people, and sometimes for buildings. That's the case with the great Crystal Palace shown in Figure 8.1. The iron and glass structure was built to host and house the Great Exhibition in London in 1851 AD. The building didn't live long; however, it left a worldwide lasting impact on architecture and building technology. All of the glass buildings we see today are simply the grandsons of the Crystal Palace. The élite building was born in London to the British royal family, Queen Victoria and Prince Albert. The happy event came as a direct reflection of the stability and prosperity that prevailed in the United Kingdom at the time. The British Empire was reaching out to its peak expansion and might. To procure the exhibition building, an international competition was held with very demanding acceptance criteria. The winner was Sir Joseph Paxton, the renowned gardener, and glasshouse architect. When completed, the stunning iron and glass Crystal Palace stole the limelight during the exhibition. In the day, it glittered like a giant diamond. In the night, it was lighting the forest like a goblet of fire.

What Makes This Project Great

The Crystal Palace marks a turning point in the history of construction and engineering of buildings representing the glory of the Industrial Revolution. Moreover, the following 10 points explain why the Crystal Palace is great by any measure or standard:

1. Marks the beginning of the modern Iron and Glass Architecture.
2. Symbolizes the might and glory of the first Industrial Revolution in the United Kingdom, forcefully.
3. Marks the beginning of modern Project Management in its finest form and shape.
4. The project's Architect, Engineer, and Contractor were knighted by the Queen.
5. Marks the first iron and glass structure built specifically for the use of people.
6. Record fast design in two weeks including detailed plans, calculations, and costing.
7. Record fast construction in 9 months including 990,000 square feet floor area.
8. Marks the beginning of the application of modular construction at large scale.
9. Marks the actual beginning or the popular World Expos that prevailed until today.
10. Still living in people's minds and inspiring architects two centuries after its disappearance.

Story Starring and Key Characters

Table 8.1 Story starring and key characters

Sir Joseph Paxton [2] 	Name	**Sir Joseph Paxton**
	Party	Independent Architect and Gardener
	Title	Chief Architect
	Legacy	A British horticulture and public gardens expert. Best known for his innovative technologies in the field of constructing glasshouses for cultivating purposes. Architect of the Crystal Palace.
	PM Role	Project Manager, Architecture
Sir William Cubitt [3] 	Name	**Sir William Cubitt**
	Party	The Great Exhibition Building Committee
	Title	Chief Engineer
	Legacy	A British civil engineer and millwright expert. Best known for his great structural engineering undertakings of his time including docks and railways. Engineer of the Crystal Palace
	PM Role	Project Manager, Engineering
Sir Charles Fox Cubitt [4] 	Name	**Sir Charles Fox**
	Party	Fox, Henderson and Co.
	Title	Construction Contractor
	Legacy	A British civil engineer and contractor. Best known for his design and construction work on railway stations, bridges, and modular structural ironwork. Builder of the Crystal Palace.
	PM Role	Project Manager, Construction

Joseph Paxton, 1803–1865 AD, is a renowned British gardener, architect, master builder, and the inventor of large-scale glasshouse construction. He was born in 1803 AD at Milton Bryan, Bedfordshire, England. Started his career in gardening field where he excelled and got famous. In 1832 AD, Joseph Paxton started developing interest in the research and development of glasshouses for horticultural purposes. A key outcome of his work was the ridge and furrow glass roofing system. In 1836 AD, Paxton was commissioned to build the Great Conservatory, a huge glasshouse in Chatsworth, which he delivered successfully in 1840 AD. His success qualified him to be entrusted in 1850 AD to construct London's 1851 AD Great Exhibition building, or the Crystal Palace, which he delivered in a spectacular fashion. On October 23, 1851 AD, Joseph Paxton was knighted by Queen Victoria in recognition of his remarkable contribution to the success of the Grand Exhibition. In 1865 AD, Sir Joseph Paxton died in his home in Sydenham at the age of 62, leaving behind a legacy as the inventor of glasshouses, which will later spread all over the word. Ironically, Paxton's marvel, the Crystal Palace, born in the Hyde Park, also died in Sydenham.

William Cubitt, 1785–1861 AD, a prominent English civil engineer and millwright. He was born in 1785 AD at Norfolk, England. William Cubitt started his civil engineering career inventing ironworks such as windmill sail and prison tread wheels. In 1826 AD, he moved to London to work on creative projects such as canal engineering, ship docks, roads, and railways. Later, William Cubitt became known for his creative mind, great experience, and for the high quality of ironwork he could produce. In January 1850 AD, William Cubitt was selected to chair the Royal Commission in charge of the London 1851 AD Great Exhibition building. William Cubitt was also appointed as the Crystal Palace's Chief Engineer. At the time, William Cubitt was the president of the UK Institution of Civil Engineers. On October 23, 1851 AD, William Cubitt was knighted by Queen Victoria in recognition of his remarkable achievements. In 1861 AD, Sir William Cubitt died at his residence in Clapham Common at the age of 76, leaving behind a remarkable legacy and appreciation.

Charles Fox, 1810–1874 AD, is an English civil engineer and ironworks construction contractor. He was born in 1810 AD at Derby, England.

Charles Fox initially had medical training, following his father's profession. In 1829 AD, he changed direction and started working on railways. He excelled in his new profession to the extent that he had his own patented inventions. In 1837 AD, he was appointed as an engineer on the London–Birmingham Railway. He later partnered with the contractor Francis Braham to form the Braham, Fox and Co contracting company. When Braham retired, the company name changed to Fox, Henderson and Co, which delivered several important projects including bridges, roofs, cranes, tanks, and permanent railway materials. In 1850 AD, the company was invited by Joseph Paxton to build the Crystal Palace for London 1851 AD Great Exhibition. On October 23, 1851 AD, Charles Fox was knighted by Queen Victoria in recognition of his remarkable achievements. In 1874 AD, Sir Charles Fox died at Blackheath, London, at the age of 64, leaving behind a sterling name and world reputation.

8.1 Exposition: Great Britain Calling the World to Fair

It's London in early 1850 AD, right after the world's first Industrial Revolution that occurred between 1760 and 1840 AD. The chiefly British Industrial Revolution introduced great inventions after almost a century of relentless work and brilliant discoveries. The UK leaders responded by calling the world to an international fair, the Great Exhibition. The event was scheduled for mid-1851 AD. Queen Victoria sent invitation to the world leaders to participate in the exhibition including colonies, dependencies, and many countries from Europe and the Americas. The Great Exhibition was meant to include the "Works of Industry of All Nations" in the industrialized or industrializing world. In January 1850 AD, a Royal Commission was established to deliver the exhibition, backed by Queen Victoria, and led by Prince Albert. Immediately upon establishment, the Royal Commission formed an executive Building Committee consisting of a number expert UK engineers and architects. The Building Committee was chaired by William Cubitt, the then president of the UK Institution of Civil Engineers. On March 15, 1850 AD, the committee invited an international competition for the exhibition building's design. The committee set a design criteria of three points, namely, simple, low cost, and possible to complete before the opening date of May 1, 1851

AD, that is practically in about a year, and then relocate. Given the significant global event, 245 local and international submissions were received in just three weeks. However, they were all rejected except for two proposals, which were also excluded for cost reasons. The most interesting proposal at this point was that of the famous architect Richard Turner, which was to cost £300,000. Proposal was deemed too expensive, hence dropped. The Building Committee, trying to find a way out of the problem, presented a design proposal of its own featuring a stone building with a huge 200 ft sheet-iron dome. The bizarre design was ridiculed by the public when posted in newspapers, so also dropped. Time was running and the situation became critical, with less than a year left to the opening date. The Grand Exhibition looked at the risk of postponement, which meant embarrassment and failure. A moment of silence and despair prevailed. This is when Joseph Paxton came into the picture with a ray of light and hope. Joseph Paxton was a renowned British gardener, known for his extensive research and experimentation of the construction of glasshouses. On June 9, 1850 AD, Sir Henry Cole, the key member of the Royal Commission, called Joseph Paxton to his office to request him to develop and submit a design proposal. Paxton accepted the request with surprise, pleasure, and enthusiasm. He left Sir Henry Cole's office and headed directly to the spot in the Hyde Park where the building was to take place. He stood starring in the air, and construction greatness appeared on the horizon.

On June 11, 1850 AD, just two days after meeting with Sir Henry Cole, Joseph Paxton came back with a genius design that will change the game and end the deadlock. A rough yet well-thought pen and ink sketch showing a glorious glasshouse building of elegant and graceful impression, as shown in Figure 8.2. Construction greatness appeared again in London's sky. An iron and glass building of modular composition and explicitly hierarchical architecture. A light structure with no bricks or mortar, no interior walls, day lighting, assemble/disassemble ability, 25 percent greater area, and best of all, cheaper and faster to construct. Moreover, the design embodied the spirit of the British industrial might and world leadership that the Great Exhibition was intended to celebrate. Sketch was admired and approved immediately by Sir Henry Cole.

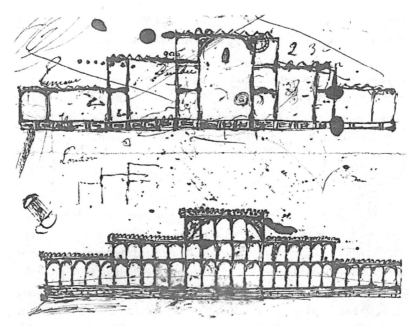

Figure 8.2 Joseph Paxton's first sketch of the Great Exhibition building [5]

Without delay, Paxton's proposal was verified by the Building Committee and deemed acceptable and fulfilling all the requirements of the competition. The design can be built fast before the opening date and its cost was estimated at £85,800, that is, only 28 percent of Richard Turner's design cost. As such, the Building Committee approved Joseph Paxton's design propos and gave it the green light to proceed with engineering and finalization.

8.2 Rising Action: Greatness in Action in a Miraculously Fast Pace

In June 1850 AD, Joseph Paxton got to work, fired with pride and enthusiasm. It's his chance to make history and the world is watching. Fast and furious, in less than two weeks, the genius Paxton turned his rough sketch into a set plan showing all basic features of the finished building, along with calculations and detailed costing. The secret behind such short design period was Paxton's application of extensive iron and glass modular construction. That concept will later lead to short construction period.

The colossal Great Exhibition building offered 990,000 ft^2 (92,000 m^2) of exhibition space. The building was two stories high with a flat-roofed rectangular hall and a large open gallery running along the main building axis with exhibition wings extending left and right. The main body of the enormous building was ca 1,851 ft (564 m) long, 408 ft (124 m) wide, along with a gorgeous central barrel-vaulted transept rising 128 ft (39 m) high. On paper, the building looked magnificent, in reality it will be formidable, glittering in the day light, and appearing in the night just like a thrilling giant ghost. So Paxton's innovative design satisfied the committee's cafeteria and added the decisive element of delight.

Joseph Paxton was neither an architect nor an engineer; however, he based his knowledge on relentless experimentation and innovation. His architectural sense and style were heavily affected by greenhouses that can control indoor temperature while letting the sunlight in to grow the plants. The ridge and furrow system invented by Paxton was easy and fast to build using modular construction in which fabrication and erection of the building elements can run progressively in parallel. No bearing walls, instead, slim hollow cast iron pillars and glass panels. Lightweight building, thus minimal foundation loads. Building engineering and structural integrity were verified and ensured by William Cubitt, the head of the Building Committee, who also acted the project's chief engineer.

As such, at this point, things looked pretty good as design was finally in hand. However, there was still one big decision to take, which is awarding the construction contract. Time is running so fast and the team is under extreme time pressure. The construction contractor will need to be able to build the project in a miraculously short time of 10 months or less, and within the estimated budget. The contractor selection was a major gamble for both Paxton and the Building Committee, win it all or lose it all. Fortunately, circumstances were in their favor as the competent contractor was available. That was the British engineering and construction company Fox, Henderson and Co led by the English civil engineer Charles Fox. The company had an excellent reputation as a capable design and construction entity, which delivered several important schemes including bridges, roofs, cranes, tanks, and railway inventions. Quickly, the company submitted a very competitive bid to build the project. In July 1850 AD, less than 10 months before the opening date, the Royal Commission approved the scheme as a whole and gave authorization to proceed with construction. Immediately, the Building Committee awarded a construction contract to Fox, Henderson and Co along with possession of the site, and construction started. The building construction involved five key integrated and interactive components, namely: (1) Foundations, (2) Cast Iron Skeleton, (3) Glass Roofs and Walls, (4) Central Barrel-Vaulted Transept, and (5) Interior Decoration and Exhibition Display Areas.

Foundations

The construction began with building a wooden fence around the site. The timber used to build the fence would later be used as flooring material for the finished building. In parallel, a subsoil investigation was conducted. Foundation works started with the setting out of the building grid identifying locations of the cast iron pillars. That was followed by casting the first batch of concrete foundations including base plates for the cast iron pillars. The concrete footings were light and shallow so completed fast making way to the installation of the building superstructure. In parallel, the drainage system was installed.

Cast Iron Skeleton

Still in parallel with the foundation construction, the fabrication of the first batches of cast iron pillars was going on. The erection of the superstructure skeleton started once the concrete foundations gained sufficient strength, and the cast iron pillars arrived to site. The erection of pillars was accompanied by the erection of the girders and rafters forming a grid of typical modular 7.3 m (24 ft) by 7.3 m (24 ft) bays. Once a number of ground floor bays were completed, the erection of the upper floor bays would follow continuously and in the same manner. Since the ironwork bays were statically determinate and self-supporting, it was possible to leave out modules in some areas, thus creating larger square- or rectangular-shaped spaces within the building to create larger exhibits, as shown in Figure 8.3. At times, the ideal just-in-time supply chain system found itself in the process, naturally. The cast iron pillars were hollow, thus lightweight, and even more creatively, being hollow, they served as down spouts to drain the rain water from the flat roofs. Lifting and maneuvering of the iron skeleton elements was done using manual hoisting equipment powered by men and horses. Painting of metal parts was carried out before erection using an inventive machine in which the metal parts are dipped into paint, then forwarded automatically to go through a system of rotating brushes to remove the excess paint. By doing that, the time and effort required to paint the metal parts after erection was eliminated. When completed, the building encompassed ca 3,300 iron pillars, 2,224 iron main girders, and other metal elements with a total of over 4,000 tons of ironwork.

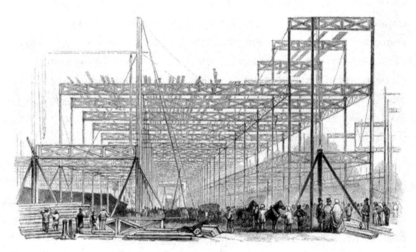

Figure 8.3 Erection of the Iron Skeleton [6]

Glass Roof and Walls

The amount of glazing works required for the building envelope was just enormous amount. Ca 900 ft² (84,000 m²) were required to be manufactured, shipped to site, and erected in just a few months. The search began for a capable glass manufacturer, which was not easy to find since glass panels manufacturing was a relatively limited industry at the time. Again, stakes went rocket high and the team held their breath. That is when Chance Brothers glassworks came into the picture offering to participate. Again, greatness appeared on the horizon. Chance Brothers glassworks was located in ca 130 km away from the site. The largest glass panels at the time measured 120 cm (49 in) long and 25 cm (10 in) wide. As such, the whole building had to be scaled around those dimensions. The identical small and light glass panes, however, were easy and fast to handle and install. That was particularity suitable for the installation of Paxton's innovative ridge and furrow roof system, shown in Figure 8.4. Glass panels were placed at 1 Vertical to 2.5 Horizontal, which allowed rays of the sunlight to pass through the glass roof most of the day, creating a delightful indoor atmosphere. The brilliant system allowed rainwater drainage through the gutters running along the furrows and flowing into the hollow cast iron pillars. It also eliminated the need for artificial lighting during the day, thus saving energy and reducing the exhibition's running cost. When completed, the building glass envelop encompassed ca 300,000 standard 120 cm × 25 cm glass panes.

Figure 8.4 *Joseph Paxton's ridge and furrow roof system* [7]

The Central Barrel-Vaulted Transept

The jewel of the crown and last major structural component remaining to be built was the central barrel-vault shaped glass transept. A semicircular arched roof that's ca 408 ft (124 m) long, 72 ft (22 m) wide/diameter, and 128 ft (39 m) high. A piece of innovative modern architecture that will last and prevail for centuries thereafter. The transept structural load carrying skeleton consisted of 16 semicircular segments. Given the time and cost limitations, the transept skeleton was made of wood, not iron. The 16 ribs were fabricated on the ground as 8 pairs and raised into position. A key aspect of the transept design was accommodating a number of large elm trees, which were feared by London environmentalists to be removed or affected. The transept design housed the old and lovely green elms letting sunlight in, as shown in Figure 8.5. The green design solution served to resolve the environmental and nature protection concerns raised by London critics.

Interior Decoration and Exhibition Display Areas

The Crystal Palace provided an enormous exhibition space. The building interior had to be as impressive as the building envelope, if not more. All works must be completed within the very limited time remaining

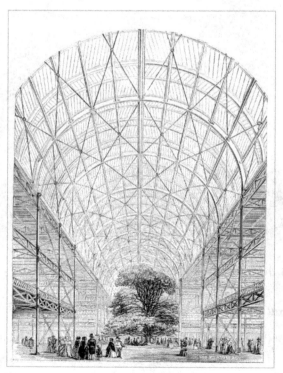

Figure 8.5 Central glass transept [8]

before the Grand Exhibition opening day. Once again, stakes went rocket high and the team found itself holding their breath. That is when Owens Jones came into the picture. Once again, greatness appeared on the horizon. Owen Jones, was an English architect, polychromy artist, and design theorist. His philosophy was affected by the Islamic art of Alhambra Palace in Granada/Spain, as well as by the ancient arts of ancient Egypt and Greece. Owen Jones was entrusted to handle the do-or-die task. He accepted the challenge and immediately got to work. Affected by ancient schemes, he chose a color palette of red, yellow, and blue for the building interior. The bizarre color scheme generated controversy and negative publicity in newspapers. Owen Jones proceeded with his work regardless, and Prince Albert showed support of the color scheme. After all, the exhibition was universal, and time was running out for the enormous. ca 990,000 ft^2 of exhibition area including over 10 miles of products display. In addition, a breathtaking 27-ft-high pink glass fountain was installed in the middle of the building. It serves to cool the atmosphere and will turn into a focal meeting point during the exhibition. Other key interior features included a police desk, areas for refreshments, waiting rooms, and in-house conveniences with private cubicles.

As is to be expected in innovation, certain issues occurred during construction. For instance, water leakage through the glass joints. Leaks were sealed with putty sealants, however persisted although at a limited manageable scale. Another technical issue was the rise in temperature inside the building. The glass envelope would let the sunray in and retain the heat. Joseph Paxton introduced a creative gravity ventilation system to mitigate the issue. The system included gear operated louvres installed in the outer walls at a high level. The louvers allowed the lighter hot air to escape and be replaced with colder air flowing through building doors. Also, the cost of construction escalated from the initially estimated £80,000 to ca £143,000. That was still way lower than the £300,000 of Richard Turner's proposal. The building cost was covered by the event income with a comfortable net profit margin. The construction of the Crystal Palace involved more than 5,000 engineers, technicians, and laborers, with 2,000 personnel active on site at peak.

By the end of April 1951 AD, the project was completed and the facility was up and running ready to impress the world. The construction of the Crystal Palace took an incredibly short period of nine months to complete, just about the period of human pregnancy.

8.3 Climax: Project Completion and Celebration

On May 1, 1851 AD, the Crystal Palace shined in the sky of the Hyde Park lighting the entire universe. The glass building glittered in the early morning's rare golden sunrays, like a giant golden diamond, broadcasting waves of positive energy, optimism, and glory. Keen, proud, and happy, Queen Victoria was there to open the Grand Exhibition—the "Great Exhibit of the Works of Industry of All Nations." The world followed the Queen into the great exhibition housed in the great and stunning Crystal Palace. Figure 8.6 shows a view of the Crystal Palace from the Knightsbridge Road of the Crystal Palace in Hyde Park. Figure 8.7 shows a view inside the building, exhibits were ready, exhibitors were on duty standing with big smiles on their faces, and sparrows of the elm trees housed under the transept filled the space with heavenly whistles and tweets. The exhibition visitors arrived in masses of all forms and shapes. Londoners and foreigners, elites in elegant carriages, commons in carts and walking, factory workers in crowds, villagers in throngs, and schoolchildren in long lines. They all came to see the display of state-of-the-art technological wonders from around the world. The exhibition included ca 100,000 objects, displayed along 10 miles of exhibition lines, and ca 15,000 exhibits from all over the world. Great Britain, as the exhibition host, occupied almost half the display space with products from the homeland, colonies, and dependencies. The rest of the exhibition was occupied by the contributing countries, especially France, Britain's worrying market competitor at the time. Toward the end of the inauguration day, a shower of fresh London rain washed off the dust from the building's glass, making the building all the more sparkling. At night, when the glass building was lit from inside, a new view appeared, nothing like that was seen before. An astonishing sight of a giant lantern, the high barrel-shaped transept in the center, and the glittering wide wings of the building spreading left and right, looking just like a giant fire ghost.

All in all, the Grand Exhibition was a great success, and the Crystal Palace itself was the most spectacular exhibition event and facility of all times. It received over 6 million visitors in about 6 months, and made ca

£186,000 of net profit. On October 11, 1851 AD, the Hyde Park Great Exhibition came to a happy end. Indeed, it entered history and will be remembered for many centuries to come. Glory to the great construction people who made this great success possible, without being mentioned by name or celebrated in person in the way they really deserve.

Figure 8.6 The Crystal Palace in Hyde Park for Grand International Exhibition of 1851 AD—external view [9]

8.4 Falling Action: Relocation, Endurance, and Disappearance

After the conclusion of the Great Exhibition, Joseph Paxton was requested to remove the exhibition building with immediate effect. The proud Crystal Palace was led to feel insulted, worthless, and unwanted. Opponents and haters welcomed the instruction. Joseph Paxton and lovers sought some time to decide on the future of the great building. Authorities wanted the Crystal Palace to disappear, at least from the Hyde Park. As the story unfolds, the crystal ghost will be forced to leave the Hyde Park with sorrow and a bleeding heart; however, will not die, since it was destined to come back to life, to appear again, shine again, and impress again. The popular Paxton managed to obtain a Parliament agreement to take time until May 1, 1952 AD to decide on the building's future. He was then quick to establish the Crystal Palace Company, then raise and provide own funds to find and buy a piece of land to

Figure 8.7 The Crystal Palace in Hyde Park for Grand International Exhibition of 1851 AD—internal view [10]

relocate the adored building to. Out of several proposed locations, Joseph Paxton chose a strategic plot located on the top of Sydenham Hill in eastern London. The chosen location was rural, however on a high hill overlooking London. A great high location for the great iconic building. The building dismantling and reconstruction job was sensibly awarded to the original building's contractor, M/s Fox, Henderson and Co. Having more time and more funds, the caring Paxton decided to take the opportunity to enhance the building design and give it more muscles. As shown in Figure 8.8, the building's main gallery was enlarged and covered with a new barrel-vaulted iron and glass roof. The central transept was also enlarged and made higher and wider. Two new transepts were added at either end of the main gallery. In addition, in order to feed major building and the numerous fountains and waterfalls surrounding the main building, two giant water towers were added to further enhance the beauty and the night of the new Crystal Palace compound. The dismantling and reconstruction of the new Crystal Palace at Sydenham Hill was completed in mid-1854 AD. On June 10, 1854 AD, Queen Victoria was once again there to open the New Crystal Palace in another historic ceremony witnessed by over 40,000 people. For decades after the second appearance, the Crystal Palace continued to be a focal point in London, housing grand exhibitions and hosting grand events. However, over the years, aging took its toll on the once young and pretty building. In 1861 AD, Prince Albert passed away at the young age of 42. A few years later, in 1865 AD, Joseph Paxton also passed away, leaving behind the great Crystal Palace all alone in the hands of the next generations. The Crystal Palace survived its creators, however like a sad and lonely old orphan. By the 1890s AD, the building's popularity and its health started to decline, significantly. That was evident in its deteriorated outer appearance, and the somewhat pathetic old fashion, old stalls, and booths. In 1901 AD, Queen Victoria passed away at the age of 82. In 1911 AD, in preparation for the Festival of the Empire held to celebrate the coronation of King George V, the wrinkly old building was given an innovation effort and a life shot. A final kiss of life. In the years after the national event, the Crystal Palace fell into despair, and disrepair. The sexy building that once was a national pride, has now become a heavy burden. Its maintenance costs were deemed unbearable. An insult, for the second time. Once again, the proud royal ghost was led to feel insulted, worthless, and unwanted. However, this time was more painful and scary. After all, all its supporters are gone. Queen Victoria, Prince Albert, Sir Henry Cole, and most of all, its inventor and best friend Sir Joseph Paxton. The Crystal Palace felt so alone, deeply injured, and trembling from fear. She decided to disappear again, in dignity, however this time, forever. Suicide. In the night of November 30, 1931 AD, an explosion was heard in the silent and empty women's cloakroom of the Crystal Palace. The small fire quickly erupted and spread all over the place turning the gigantic building into a huge goblet of fire, as shown in Figure 8.9. All the sincere efforts of the over 400 firemen failed to make the ghost change her mind or get back to life. The Crystal Palace set itself on fire with great determination aided by the winds of fate, which were there on time to blow on Sydenham Hill. Over 100,000 Londoners rushed to Sydenham Hill to watch the blaze. Among the audience was the famous British politician Winston Churchill, who was quoted to say, "This is the end of an age" (White, R.; Yorath, J. 2004). Indeed. At dawn the next morning, all what could be seen from the all-time glorious Crystal Palace were ruins, dust, and debris. Tears. RIP.

Figure 8.8 The Crystal Palace after relocation to Sydenham Hill [11]

Figure 8.9 The Crystal Palace at Sydenham Hill set on fire [12]

8.5 Resolution: The Crystal Palace Today

Today, the Crystal Palace is in heaven, except that it might come back to life. You look up into the sky, and she is looking down at you. You look up the Internet, and she is all over the place. The Londoner Crystal Palace is just one of us. Just like humans, she was built and born in nine months. She had a loving mother, Queen Victoria, and a caring Dad, Prince Albert. The Crystal Palace was born on May 1, 1851 AD in the Hyde Park, London, and then moved to Sydenham Hill, London, to grow up. She lived a life that's full, before getting old and ill, and committing a heartbreaking suicide the very night of November 30, 1936 AD. She passed away at the young age of 85. The Crystal Palace graveyard at Sydenham Hill is still empty, despite several plans and attempts to try and revive the glorious iron and glass palace. Numerous proposals were made by various groups to revive and reconstruct the Crystal Palace in Sydenham Hill; however, none of them come to fruition. It would appear that the dignified ghost is still angry because of the neglect and humiliation it had witnessed from people late in its life. Great buildings demand respect and admiration to live and persist. Or, I reckon, it might be waiting for someone to propose putting it up in its original cradle location, in the Hyde Park. I remember when I visited London for the first time in 2005, I went directly to the Hyde Park looking for the Crystal Palace. At the time, I had no idea about the full story, and couldn't understand what they were talking about when they told me that the palace was not available. Now I understand. The architecture of the Crystal Palace is just unforgettable and irreplaceable. In the immediate term effect right after the Great Exhibition, the Crystal Palace set an architectural standard for the following international exhibitions, which likewise adopted iron and glass building. That included immediate successors—the Cork Exhibition of 1852 AD, the Dublin and New York City expositions of 1853 AD, and the Munich Exhibition of 1854 AD. In the long-term effect, despite its sad departure almost a century ago, the Crystal Palace is still living in people's collective memory, inspiring architects and entrepreneurs all over the world. Numerous buildings had tried to mimic or follow the style and footsteps of the Crystal Palace; however, none of them came nearly close to its unmatchable impact and glory. On the other hand, the influences of the Crystal Palace on today's building practices are inevitable and plenty including structural frames, standard metal roll-up shapes, prefabricated steel buildings, and indeed the entire project management discipline as a whole. Glory to the Crystal Palace, its parents Queen Victoria and Prince Albert in Figure 8.10, its steward Joseph Paxton, and all its known and unknown leaders, architects, engineers, technicians, and workers. Glory to the heroes and martyrs of construction greatness who worked hard to give us the fulfillment and inspiration we have today. Remembering the Crystal Palace, living its story, starring at its façade, and walking around it and through its corridors, exhibits, stalls, fountains, and hallways. The world is waiting for the comeback of the Crystal Palace, the royal ghost that appeared twice before vanishing in the flames.

Figure 8.10 Queen Victoria of the Queen of the United Kingdom [13] and her Husband Prince Albert of Saxe-Coburg and Gotha [14]

Story Recap Illustrated on Story Plot Diagram

The following Figure 8.11 provides overview and recap of the story spread along the five components of the typical story telling plot diagram, namely, Exposition, Rising Action, Climax, Falling Action, and Resolution.

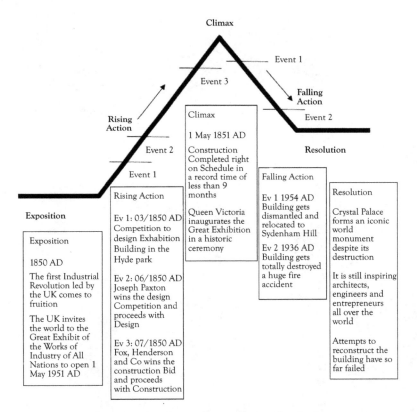

Figure 8.11 The crystal palace story on story plot diagram

Taj Mahal Mausoleum, Agra, India—The Story of Emperor Shah Jahan and His Teardrop on the Face of Eternity

It's 1631 AD in Agra, Uttar Pradesh, India.

The Mughal Emperor loses his beloved Empress. The heart-broken widower falls into deep remorse, then decides to turn his eternal love into an eternal mausoleum. The mausoleum had to reflect both the greatness of his love and the unrivaled beauty of his adored wife. The outcome was a teardrop on the face of eternity.

Figure 9.1 Taj Mahal mausoleum, Agra, India [1]

Table of Contents

Preface

At times, construction greatness can spring from the heart of pain. Greatness is a great event that doesn't seem to happen under normal circumstances and calm winds. That is exactly the case in the story of the Taj Mahal mausoleum. The enchanting story of love, loss, remorse, sorrow, and pain turning into vision, energy, creativity, glory, and making history. Almost five centuries after its construction, the Taj Mahal mausoleum is still standing sturdy, sad, and beautiful with charm, majesty, and charisma. Telling the world its heart-melting story that's one of a kind in human history. Representing construction greatness in its full definition and designation. If Taj Mahal is not construction greatness, what another building in the world would be? Simple, robust, mesmerizing, unshaken, and eye-catching. Taj Mahal is the world's only monument of pure matrimonial love and loyalty of a man to his wife. No surprise the ancient monument completed in 1654 AD was voted by one hundred million people in 2007 AD to be on the list of the World's New Seven Wonders. No wonder it is still attracting millions of visitors each year whether believers, architects, artists, world leaders, celebrities, or lovers. After all, who can come up with a better or greater monument that's backed up with a genuine story of the love of an Emperor to his Empress, and funded by resources of an entire empire? The Emperor accesses the throne, the Empress dies, and the story begins.

What Makes This Project Great

The Taj Mahal mausoleum is a distinguished landmark in the history of human architecture of buildings representing the glory of Indo-Islamic art. Moreover, the following 10 points explain why Taj Mahal mausoleum is great by any measure or standard:

1. On the new list of the "New Seven Wonders of the World" voted by 100 million people.
2. Taj Mahal site attracts seven to eight million visitors a year from all over the world.
3. It is widely considered as the best example for Indo-Islamic Mughal architecture.
4. A perfect example symbol of India's rich culture, architecture, and construction history.
5. One of the universally admired masterpieces of the world's heritage.
6. The world's only monument to have been built to honor the love of a man to his wife.
7. Its design sheer grandeur makes it one of the most arresting man-made monuments.
8. The all four direction symmetry symbolizes stability and glory of the Mughal Empire.
9. A unique world heritage symbol and inspiration of matrimonial love and devotion.
10. A designated UNESCO World Heritage Site since 1983 AD.

Story Starring and Key Characters

Table 9.1 Story starring and key characters

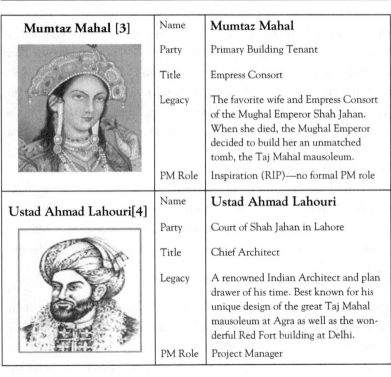

Shah Jahan[2]	Name	**Shah Jahan**
	Party	Owner and Developer
	Title	The Fifth Mughal Emperor
	Legacy	The fifth Mughal Emperor. His reign witnessed a golden era of Indo-Islamic architecture. Best known for the Taj Mahal mausoleum he built for his beloved wife Mumtaz Mahal.
	PM Role	Project Sponsor

Mumtaz Mahal [3]	Name	**Mumtaz Mahal**
	Party	Primary Building Tenant
	Title	Empress Consort
	Legacy	The favorite wife and Empress Consort of the Mughal Emperor Shah Jahan. When she died, the Mughal Emperor decided to build her an unmatched tomb, the Taj Mahal mausoleum.
	PM Role	Inspiration (RIP)—no formal PM role

Ustad Ahmad Lahouri[4]	Name	**Ustad Ahmad Lahouri**
	Party	Court of Shah Jahan in Lahore
	Title	Chief Architect
	Legacy	A renowned Indian Architect and plan drawer of his time. Best known for his unique design of the great Taj Mahal mausoleum at Agra as well as the wonderful Red Fort building at Delhi.
	PM Role	Project Manager

Shah Jahan, or King of the World, 1592–1666 AD, is the fifth Indian Emperor in the ancient Mughal Empire. In 1628 AD, the powerful Indian prince succeed his father Emperor Jahangir after a fierce competition with his brothers. In a short time of his reign, the Mughal Empire reached its peak of might and stability. That was marked by many a grand buildings put up in his era. Emperor Shah Jahan is most known for developing the remarkable Taj Mahal mausoleum. He built it as a memorial for his beloved wife Mumtaz Mahal who passed away in 1631 AD. In 1657 AD, Shah Jahan got seriously ill. In 1666 AD, he passed away at the age of 74 leaving behind a bright legacy of great building, culture, architecture, and an all-time human story of immortal matrimonial love. Shah Jahan was laid to rest in the Taj Mahal mausoleum next to his beloved wife Empress Mumtaz Mahal in a unique occurrence in human history.

Mumtaz Mahal, or the Exalted-One of the Palace, 1593–1631 AD, is Emperor Shah Jahan's favorite wife and Emperor Consort. She was born to a noble and wealthy Persian family. In 1612 AD, at the age of 19 years, she got married to Prince Shahab-ud-din Muhammad Khurram, then 20 years old, who would be later named Emperor Shah Jahan. The young couple had a happy life and 14 children. Empress Mumtaz Mahal died in 1631 AD at the young age of 38 while giving birth to her 14th child from Emperor Shah Jahan. Her departure was a devastating event, which broke the Emperor's heart and changed his life forever. In response, the grieving Emperor Shah Jahan instructed the construction of the Taj Mahal mausoleum to honor his beloved wife. The mausoleum will later become a world monument and unique symbol of matrimonial devotion and undying love.

Ustad Ahmad Lahouri, 1580–1649 AD, is a prominent Persian Architect and Master Builder of the Mughal Empire era. He began his fame and legacy during the fourth Mughal Empire, then carried on well into the fifth Empire under Emperor Shah Jahan. Ustad Ahmad Lahori's legacy include the Red Fort at Delhi completed in 1648 AD. His jewel of the crown however remains the Taj Mahal mausoleum he completed between 1632 and 1652 AD. He worked under the direct supervision and command of Emperor Shah Jahan. Ustad Ahmad Lahori's architectural school introduced a combination of the spiritual Indo-Islamic architecture and the strong royal style of the Mughal Empire reflecting strength and supremacy. In 1649 AD, he died peacefully at the age of 69 years leaving behind a great legacy.

9.1 Exposition: Emperor's Accession to the Throne and Empress Demise

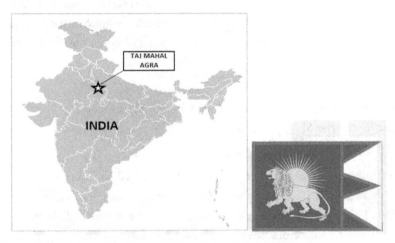

Figure 9.2 Map of India and Flag of the Mughal Empire [5][6]

It's the early 1600s AD in Agra, Uttar Pradesh, India. The Mughal Empire is reaching its peak in terms of glory, power, resources, expansion, maturity, and stability (Figure 9.2). In 1627 AD, the fourth Mughal Emperor Jahangir passes away leaving behind a strong and vast Empire. In 1628 AD, the "survival of the fittest" rule applies and the capable prince Shahab-ud-din Muhammad Khurram conquers his competitors, succeeds his father, accesses the throne, calls himself Shah Jahan or king of the world, and becomes the fifth Mughal Emperor. The new Emperor was obviously a different character from tradition warrior-like Emperors. He had a unique personality combining strength and leadership with artistic mind and romantic heart full of love for his favorite wife Mumtaz Mahal, or the exalted one of the palace. He further named her his Empress Consort as a gesture of full gratitude and devotion. His life looked great that moment and everything seemed to be alright. All of a sudden, fate strikes. In 1631 AD, three years into the young monarchy, the magnificent Empress Consort dies while giving birth to her 14th child. The loving husband Emperor gets devastated. He wanted to honor his beloved wife, and he did it in his own way, through art and architecture. He instructed to build her an unrivaled tomb, a splendid mausoleum that the whole world will keep staring at forever. Style had to be Mughal Indo-Islamic, and unlike common red stone buildings of the time, the mausoleum had to stand out and be white marble. Symbol of pureness and eternity. As to be expected from a loving Emperor to tribute his wholehearted beloved wife, the construction project budget was open and so was project delivery time. And design and construction begin.

9.2 Rising Action: Clouds of Construction Greatness Gather in the Skies of Agra

In 1631 AD, shortly after Empress Mumtaz Mahal's death, Emperor Shah Jahan appointed the renowned Mughal Chief Architect Ustad Ahmad Lahouri to design and deliver the mausoleum. Immediately, Ustad Ahmad Lahouri put everything aside and got fully dedicated to work on the Emperor's project. The mandate was to turn the Emperor's vision of greatness and beauty into reality. To do that, he needed to activate all the creativity and confidence in the world. Taj Mahal, or crown of the palace, had to be everything. At the very least, it had to be an unseen and unmatched masterpiece of architecture and grandeur, to the powerful and sorrowed Mughal Emperor's satisfaction. And, from the onset, the chief architect had to work under the direct day-to-day command and direction of the smart and talented Emperor. A team of the world's best architects, engineers, artists, technicians, and skilled laborers of the time were called in to participate in the Mughal Emperor's top priority project. Experts gathered from everywhere in the world; showers of beauty and greatness fell on the fields of Agra. India and the Mughal Empire with significant contributions by top-talent craftsmen from Persia and the Ottoman Empire. Numerous experts came to participate in the delivery of the imperial project at one point or another along its project life span.

Architectural Design and Scheme

In 1632 AD, the great Chief Architect Ustad Ahmad Lahouri started to draft his first design lines. A horizontal ground line, a vertical axis of symmetry, and, inspired by the sadness and soreness of the grieving Emperor, a slightly flattened tear-drop-like circle marking the mausoleum's central dome. Step by step, the mausoleum elements and features started to appear, as shown in Figures 9.3 and 9.4. A grand massive central dome symbol of grandeur and greatness, four smaller domes and four slim and high minarets symbolizing the four key schools of thought in Islam, and a great high gate entryway stirring fear and symbolizing the status of the tenants. The mausoleum was designed to be strictly symmetrical as shown in Figure 9.5, symbolizing sovereignty and correctness. The common color of building facades used in great forts and worship houses at the time was red. However, the brilliant and miserable Emperor Shah Jahan decided a departure from the norm and insisted to stand out with a white building façade made of white marble. White color being a symbol of peace, pureness, and eternity. The outcome was a revolutionary design and a masterpiece of modern architecture. The four mausoleum elevations were seen the same from all four directions, and that's a key part of the building's architectural genuineness. A style that is combining the ancient Hindu art and the spiritual Islamic architecture, art, and culture. The central cenotaph chamber took an octagonal shape, a trademark feature of the Islamic art. The Taj Mahal mausoleum's majestic and mysterious style marked the birth of a new Indo-Islamic architectural impression that would later on prevail in the Mughal Empire and the entire India and Persia, taking various shapes and forms. So once the mausoleum's architecture design concept was approved by Emperor Shah Jahan, engineering design and construction were ready to start and proceed in parallel, in a way similar to the nowadays modern design–build construction process.

Choosing Project Location

Taj Mahal mausoleum's location had to be outstanding. As outstanding, sacred, and great as the building itself. The chosen location was therefore not an easy feat. After due consideration, the mausoleum location was chosen right in a strategic spot. That was in an exclusive area of elite gardens

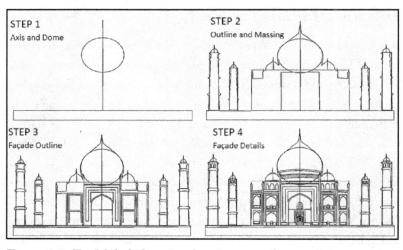

Figure 9.3 Taj Mahal elevation drawing—step by step [7]

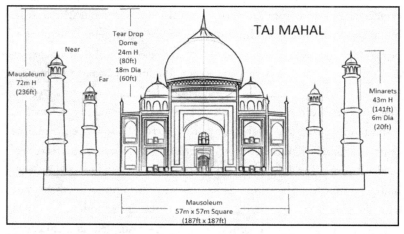

Figure 9.4 Taj Mahal mausoleum—elevation and key dimensions [7]

and palaces of the prominent Mughals located in eastern Agra, the capital of the great Mughal Empire at the time. Site location was so close to and right on the banks of the Yamuna River, the sacred river and basin of human purification from sin in the Hindu culture. The building location, embracing gardens and rivers, also resembled the glorious afterlife eternal paradise according to the Islamic faith. From a construction perspective, locating the building close to a river was advantageous as it enables river shipping of the construction materials to the construction site. On the

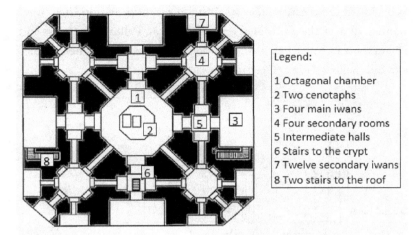

Figure 9.5 Taj Mahal mausoleum—plan view [8]

other hand, locating the building on the silt and clay river bank imposed a challenge to the design and construction of the building foundation.

Substructure Works—Deep Foundations and Soil Stabilization

Later in 1632 AD, the construction of the Taj Mahal mausoleum began. The first major challenge faced by the project team was building a solid foundation for the massive building. The close proximity of the building site to the Yamuna River imposed a risk of foundation settlement and instability. That task was particularly challenging, due to the poor subsoil conditions involving the top layers of soft clay. Resting the building on the top of the shallow layer of compressive soft clay shall entail excessive settlement due to long-term consolidation, leading to building failure. The clever Ustad Ahmad Lahouri and the engineering team realized such risk and decided to go for deep foundations. They dug deep wells of bulged tips, supported by wooden shoring, then filled up such wells with stone and mortar concrete. That foundation system, shown in Figure 9.6, consisted of an array of vertical rigid piles that can transfer the heavy superstructure loads down to the deep stiff clay layer or bearing strata. Once the piling works was completed and the concrete piles gained sufficient strength, the construction of the superstructure was ready to begin. In the meantime, as a soil stabilization provision, trees were planted all over the Taj Mahal complex area and allowed to grow and extend roots in parallel with construction. That served to further stabilize soft and shallower top soil layers.

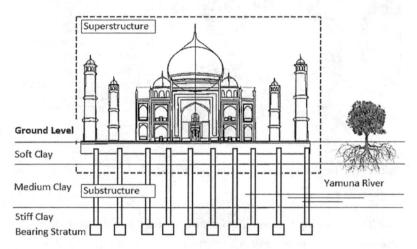

Figure 9.6 Taj Mahal mausoleum—piled foundations and soil stabilization

Superstructure Works—Walls, Slabs, Domes, Facades, and Minarets

In 1632 AD, the substructure foundation was completed. In parallel with that, design of the superstructure was largely finalized and superstructure construction was ready to start. Still in parallel, a large amount of the sandstone and mudbrick blocks was manufactured and procured to the site to build the mausoleum walls. As such, the construction of the massive mausoleum brick walls and mortar started right away early on and proceeded expeditiously. An innovative pulley system was invented and used to raise the heavy wall blocks to the desired positions. In the meantime, with a short start-to-start lag, the construction of the four corner Minarets taking place around the mausoleum began. As construction progressed, the minarets started projecting high in the air announcing the beginning of completion of the legendary Taj Mahal mausoleum. Two key downstream finish-to-start activities were waiting for the completion of wall construction to kick start. The first activity was the installation of the mausoleum's white marble façade wall cladding. A very expensive and time-consuming work item, which was insisted upon by the powerful and sorrowed Emperor Shan Jahan. The large white marble panels were sourced from Makrana, the marble city of India, located almost 300 km to the north-west of Agra. A major earth ramps was built and used to transport construction materials up to the construction site level. Figure 9.7 shows a site overview of the Taj Mahal mausoleum under construction. Construction cost started to go rocket high. Construction budget was however merely open, and all costs were just to be charged to the imperial treasury.

Figure 9.7 Taj Mahal mausoleum—under construction [9]

The other key downstream activity that followed the completion of the mausoleum walls was the Taj Mahal central and focal dome. The tear drop dome. The unique dome that will later become a world treasure and part of the global art and human sentiment. The key task required calling in a dome design and construction expert from the Ottoman Empire, namely, Architect Mehmet Ismail Effendi. The dome design was unprecedented and its accurate construction took substantial amount of time, focus, and expertise. The construction of the building roofs and domes construction used sturdy scaffolding system made of bamboos and temporary brick structures. When construction was completed, and in order to get rid of the large amount of temporary works bricks, the smart Emperor Shah Jahan used a creative method to get that done. He offered that whoever takes such bricks away can keep it. Since such bricks were kind of sacred and were of good quality, bricks were ripped to pieces and taken off site by local peasants overnight.

Calligraphy and Decorative Works

By 1639 AD, the main construction works of the mausoleum were completed. Calligraphic and decorative works however continued for more than a decade beyond that point. Solid works were the body and the soul, calligraphy and decoration were the lyrics and facial expressions. Calligraphic inscriptions were assigned to the prominent Persian artist of the time Abd-ul-Haqq, branded as Amanat Khan, or the Trustworthy, assisted by a vast team of highly skilled craftsmen. The main decorative artwork style adopted in the mausoleum was flowery and vegetative themes symbolizing paradise, in addition to calligraphic inscriptions of Arabic verses and passages of the holy Quran, as shown in Figure 9.9. The reason for that was that the Islamic religion and culture strictly prohibits the use of human or animal images or statues. That constraint, however, opened doors to matchless excellence and creativity in the design and application of calligraphic inscriptions. Script was mostly made of verses and passages of the holy Quran written in Arabic on walls and doors. Inscriptions were made of black marble used both to decorate and to spread the Islamic message of monotheism. Several types of precious and semiprecious stones and marbles were used to create the flower and plants. Calligraphic inscriptions were carved and painted in marbles and doors. Fortunately, the genius Amanat Khan was allowed to put his name and date on his work. That allowed tracing the chronology and sequence of calligraphic works, which was starting from the top down. The last inscriptions were those on the mausoleum's main door reading: "Finished with His help, the Most High, 1057." The number 1057 is the Hijri lunar calendar corresponding to 1647 AD. In 1648 AD, the great Amanat Khan passed away leaving behind a whole school of calligraphic art and a great legacy of unique artistic calligraphy.

A few years later, the construction of the entire Taj Mahal mausoleum and complex including ancillary buildings and landscape works was completed. All in all, construction of the 42-acre complex extended over about 22 years and was completed in bits and pieces, phases and stages. Construction cost was estimated at 32 million rupees at the time, or USD 1 billion in 2021 AD. A mammoth cost, however trivial when compared to Emperor Shah Jahan's love to his beloved wife Mumtaz Mahal, or to his endless melancholy for her departure. No time or cost pressure or stress was felt or reported, only hard work, high focus, and great commitment to quality and superiority of the end-product. Over 20,000 laborers, designers, builders, technicians, masons, stonecutters, artists, and painters participated in making Taj Mahal happen. In addition, over 1,000 elephants and oxen were deployed to support the transportation, lifting, and handling of heavy construction materials, and they did a great job. Glory to the martyrs of construction greatness who spent or lost their lives to make this great project happen. The outcome was a great monument that will keep the world staring at it for many centuries to come.

9.3 Climax: Project Completion and Celebration

In 1654 AD, Taj Mahal shined in the sky of the universe along the Yamuna, the river of death and purity. As shown in Figure 9.8, beautiful but lonely and sad, glorious but heartbreaking and tear-jerking. The central dome looked like a big tear drop, surrounded by smaller domes of tear drops. The white mausoleum looked like a bloodless dead body and façade arches resembled narrow vents to a box of death, remorse, and sorrow. The mausoleum's main gate, however, bore the sign of hope, optimism, and faith. Divine verses of the Holy Quran and floral patterns resembling the eternal paradise, are as shown in Figure 9.9. The tear drop mausoleum didn't end the widower's pain, and nothing would do. It's a pity that the huge cost of the legendary mausoleum was only invested to commemorate and tribute death, and not to enjoy or celebrate life. As to be expected, there was no project completion celebration on that day. Only further grief and a second burial and funeral ceremony. Once construction was completed, the body of the Empress Mumtaz Mahal was moved to the mausoleum's lower burial chamber. A beautiful cenotaph of the Empress elevated on a pedestal was placed right in the center of the octagonal chamber located in the center of the mausoleum building. Emperor Shah Jahan then wanted to build a duplicate of Taj Mahal for himself but in black marble to further express his sadness. However, this time his dream was never realized as he got seriously ill and ousted from power in 1658 AD. In 1666 AD, Emperor Shah Jahan died at the age of 74. He got buried in Taj Mahal lower tomb next to his beloved wife. A second cenotaph was added for the Emperor in the central octagonal chamber right next to Empress Mumtaz Mahal's. And life went on, and so did death and history.

Figure 9.8 Taj Mahal complex at completion—overview [10]

Figure 9.9 Taj Mahal mausoleum—gate calligraphy and decoration [11]

9.4 Falling Action: Popularity Grows and Firmness Persists Despite the Ages

A few decades after Emperor Shah Jahan's era, the Mughal Empire started to decline down the road of the 17th century. Over the years and under the weaker Emperors, the once mighty empire started to lose power and territories gradually. That scenario continued to the point that, in the 18th century, Agra, the city of Taj Mahal, got invaded by the Jat rulers of the Kingdom of Bharatpur of Northern India. The invaders attacked the Taj Mahal mausoleum and looted it, however without causing significant harm to the mausoleum building itself. Nevertheless, time and lack of maintenance did some harm to the building, although of a limited scale. After all, the mausoleum was built by the best engineers of the time, using the strongest materials, and best of all was deep founded. Deep and piled foundations protect buildings from cracking due to foundation settlement or differential settlement, common in shallow-founded buildings resting on weak soils. Given the moral value of Taj Mahal and its Islamic style, Muslim rulers and people in the region kept it unharmed, and indeed loved it and appreciated it. Still, time took its toll on the building after over two centuries in service. In 1856 AD, the British started to rule India. In late the 19th century, a comprehensive restoration project of the Taj Mahal complex and its gardens was carried out and completed in 1908 AD. The restoration was mainly cosmetic, since the building was largely intact. It focused on gardens and introduced trivial items to the mausoleum such as a large lamp to the interior chamber. Otherwise, all in all, Taj Mahal mausoleum reserved its original components, style, and impression without deterioration or improvement. And that is the wonder of it.

9.5 Resolution: The Taj Mahal Mausoleum Today

Today, Taj Mahal is standing high and proud at the forefront of popular ancient monuments in the world. You show its picture to anyone anywhere and you hear, "Ah, Taj Mahal." Today, Taj Mahal has become a first-class tourism point attracting over 8 million visitors a year from India and all over the world. All the way from tourists to peasants, believers, architects, artists, royals, presidents, and celebrities. In 1983 AD, Taj Mahal was designated as a UNESCO World Heritage Site, and labeled "the jewel of Muslim art in India and one of the universally admired masterpieces of the world's heritage." In 2007, for many good reasons confirmed by feedback from millions people around the world, Taj Mahal was declared a winner of the New Seven Wonders of the World. Nowadays, Taj Mahal is in a very good structural condition, showing no signs of dilatation or structural distress. Taj Mahal is however facing two major risks, namely, mass tourism and air pollution. Mass tourism accelerates the aging wear and tear effects naturally and inevitably occur to building as a result of the heavy rate of use. And, the air pollution caused by motor vehicles, which accelerates the degradation of the white marble façade, the lapidary inlays, and the building decorations in general. In order to mitigate such risks, the Indian government is imposing a range of proactive measures to protect the building, including restrictions on road traffic and strict guidelines for tourists. All in all, Taj Mahal is currently in good hands and in good health. As shown in Figure 9.10, Taj Mahal of Agra/India, is still standing, firm and proud, sad and beautiful, with charm and majesty, telling the world about the great love story of Emperor Shah Jahan and Empress Mumtaz Mahal.

Figure 9.10 The Emperor, the Taj Mahal mausoleum, and the Empress [12]

Story Recap Illustrated on Story Plot Diagram

The following Figure 9.11 provides overview and recap of the story spread along the five components of the typical story telling plot diagram, namely, Exposition, Rising Action, Climax, Falling Action, and Resolution.

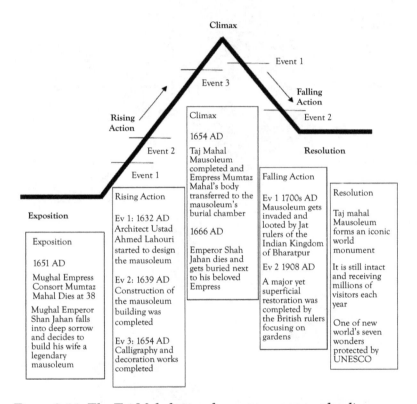

Figure 9.11 The Taj Mahal mausoleum story on story plot diagram

CHAPTER 10

Project Management Lessons Learned

Greatness can best be repeated if we learn from lessons of the past.
Great ancient projects generated a substantial body of knowledge which
needs to be documented and reserved. That is for the new and future
generations of great builders to pick up from their great master builder
ancestors, and take forward the torch of construction greatness.

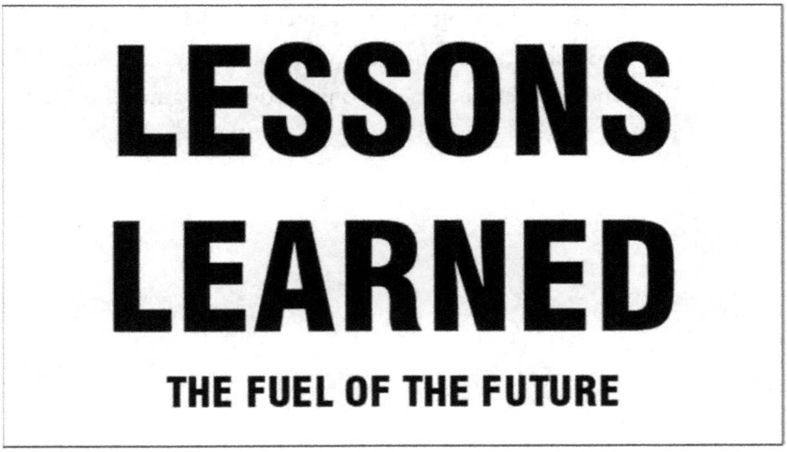

LESSONS LEARNED

THE FUEL OF THE FUTURE

Figure 10.1 Lessons learned—the fuel of the future

Table of Contents

Preface

Greatness has secrets, and secrets are usually not revealed or announced, but extracted and discovered. In this chapter, the eight great project stories are reviewed and analyzed aiming to extract and reveal secrets of construction greatness. That is accomplished by running project proceedings through three of the most famous modern project management schools, namely PMI, Agile, and Design–Build. Through reflecting on project proceedings with key project management methods in mind, lessons learned shine and key wisdoms reveal. The PMI project management school is concerned with the project team, project life cycle, project management knowledge areas, and recently with value delivery and project management principles. The Agile project management school looks into the fundamental timeless relationship between service providers and clients and the progressive nature of projects while progressing toward completion. And, the Design–Build project management school focuses on satisfying customer requirements through the selection of the best design and construction solutions, and on fast-tracking design and construction activities. The big picture is not entirely clear until all project stories, reviews, and analysis are read and absorbed. Moreover, not until the reader reflects on own experiences and makes own sense of the information provided. That is when one starts to see and discover the magical pathway leading to construction greatness. As mentioned in Figure 10.1, lessons learned are the fuel of the future.

10.1 Lessons Learned Using PMI PMBOK® Guide Project Management Model

10.1.1 Introduction

PMI, or the Project Management Institute (www.pmi.org), is the world's leading professional association in the field of modern project management. The most popular PMI product is the PMI PMBOK® Guide, or the Project Management Body of Knowledge Guide. The early editions of the PMBOK® Guide up to the sixth edition (PMI 2017) introduced a project management framework that is focusing on project delivery. The framework focused on the project management team, the project life cycle, and 10 project management knowledge areas (KAs). Recently, a revamped seventh edition of the PMBOK® Guide (PMI 2021) was issued shifting the focus to value delivery and introducing a project management system consisting of 5 project management areas, and 12 project management principles. This section provides a project management review and analysis of the great project stories based on both the earlier and the current approaches of the PMI PMBOK® Guide.

10.1.2 Chapter 2 Pharaoh Djoser's Step Pyramid, Saqqara, Egypt

PMBOK® Guide 6th Edition Project Management Review, Analysis, and Lessons Learned

> **PROJECT SPONSOR:** Project is sponsored by a king, namely, Pharaoh Djoser. Great projects require strong sponsors with authority and ability to provide resources.

> **PROJECT MANAGER:** Imhotep, who was a polymath, so his background in various knowledge areas enabled him to innovate and shine, e.g. architecture, stone making, and chemistry.

> **PROJECT TEAM:** Local farmers and skilled workers of various disciplines who were motivated by the project's royal and devout purpose, akin 'spiritual project management'.

INITIAL	INTERMEDIATE	FINAL

> **KA01 PROJECT INTEGRATION MANAGEMENT**
>
> Project benefitted from having Imhotep as a great mastermind in control of the project's technical and logistical aspects. Greatness requires strong project integration.

PROJECT INITIATION	KA02 SCOPE MGMT	KA03 TIME MGMT	KA04 COST MGMT	PROJECT CLOSING
Strong and swift start is key. Imhotep's instant start of the initial mastaba satisfied Djoser and enabled an early quick win.	It's key to be swift in applying design changes, e.g. scope change P1 to P2	Continuous flow of design information to construction is crucial	Using labor of farmers idle during flooding times cut cost significantly	Strong and ritual finish is key. Imhotep's timely completion before Djoser's death and grand celebration were a big success.
	KA05 QUALITY MGMT	**KA06 HR MGMT**	**KA07 COMM MGMT**	
	Excellent stone quality of consistent sizes facilitated construction	The Spiritual motivation of construction workers boosted productivity	Effective communication between designer and construction	
	KA08 RISK MGMT	**KA09 PROC MGMT**	**KA10 STAKEHOLDERS**	
	High location to reduce risk of floods, and deep shaft to reduce risk of theft.	Digging a nearby trench as a source of stones was a perfect proc decision	Excellent management of stakeholders from Pharaoh to Workers	

PMBOK® Guide 7th Edition Project Management Review, Analysis, and Lessons Learned

THE NEW STANDARD FOR PROJECT MANAGEMENT 2021

A SYSTEM FOR VALUE DELIVERY				
ASFVD-01 **CREATING VALUE**	ASFVD-02 **GOVERN- ANCE**	ASFVD-03 **PM FUNC- TIONS**	ASFVD-04 **ENVIRON- MENT**	ASFVD-05 **PRODUCT MGMT**
Can best be realized by first satisfying project goal, a safe tomb, then boosters, inventive design and world's tallest building status.	Done by a highly author- ized PM in a design-build setting, e.g. approvals of creative design, first use of stone, size change.	Sound plan- ning is key to success, e.g. standardizing stone sizes, resources surge during floods, and applying special stone expertise.	A combined favorable internal and external envi- ronment can boost value, e.g. Int vast resources and Ext political stability.	Value can be boosted through adding functions, e.g. a mortuary complex and burial chambers for royal family members.

PROJECT MANAGEMENT PRINCIPLES			
PMP-01 **STEWARDSHIP**	PMP-02 **TEAM COLLAB**	PMP-03 **STAKEHOLDERS**	PMP-04 **VALUE**
Appointing a strong trusted PM can ensure strong stew- ardship e.g. a Vizier Imhotep.	Spiritual and nation- al missions promote team motivation and collaboration.	PM continuous liaison with the Client is key to project success, e.g. Imhotep to Pharaoh.	Monitoring client expectations, e.g. pyramid size, was key to value delivery.
PMP-05 **SYSTEMS THINK- ING**	PMP-06 **LEADERSHIP**	PMP-07 **TAILORING**	PMP-08 **QUALITY**
Evident in the dovetailing sub- and superstructure subsystems	Superior leadership can be achieved by actuating national and spiritual motiva- tions	Standardization process can be key to productivity, e.g. standard stone sizes.	Selecting the right material is key, e.g. stone of steady qual- ity in lieu of mud bricks
PMP-09 **COMPLEXITY**	PMP-10 **OPTIMIZE RISK**	PMP-11 **ADAPT/RESIL- IENCE**	PMP-12 **ENABLE CHANGE**
Complexity can be a project necessity requiring skill, e.g. maze of burial tunnels.	Risk avoidance can be the best way, e.g. pyramid lo- cated high to avoid groundwater.	Exhausting work over many years endured by the team, e.g. tunneling in stone.	Change can be the way to achieve the desired outcome, e.g. pyramid size change.

10.1.3 Chapter 3 The Empire State Building, New York City, USA

PMBOK® Guide 6th Edition Project Management Review, Analysis, and Lessons Learned

---

PROJECT SPONSOR: Project is sponsored by John J Raskob, a politician and businessman. Delivering great projects requires both political and financial support.

PROJECT MANAGER: William Lamb leading design from concept to details; and William Starrett leading construction from excavation to handover, in harmony and alliance.

PROJECT TEAM: Skilled labors and technicians from Starrett Brothers and Eken Inc., including the brave construction workers who worked at the very height so nicknamed 'Sky Boys'.

INITIAL INTERMEDIATE FINAL

KA01 PROJECT INTEGRATION MANAGEMENT

John Raskob took full ownership of project integration. That included setting goals, securing funds, selecting project team, interface management, and providing leadership.

PROJECT INITIATION	KA02 SCOPE MGMT	KA03 TIME MGMT	KA04 COST MGMT	PROJECT CLOSING
Starting site work while design is still at concept stage was a great decision which turned the project into design–build although with two separate entities.	Adding 16 floors early on to be way higher than Chrysler enabled scope stability.	Linear scheduling is good for High-rise buildings construction	Building in time of recession can reduce construction cost due to deflation	Completion should overlap with proper media coverage and marketing efforts to ensure adequate project announcement and profitability.
	KA05 QUALITY MGMT	KA06 HR MGMT	KA07 COMM MGMT	
	The Use of prefabricated elements rises quality due to factory controls	Using Skilled And motivated labor can do wonders as the Sky Boys did	Just-in-time delivery was key to success and required superb comm skills	
	KA08 RISK MGMT	KA09 PROC MGMT	KA10 STAKEHOLD-ERS	
	Loosing race risk managed via extra height, and recession used to advantage.	Just-in-time procurement reduces storage and improves cash flow	Investor, authorities, suppliers, media, designers, and builders	

PMBOK® Guide 7th Edition Project Management Review, Analysis, and Lessons Learned

THE NEW STANDARD FOR PROJECT MANAGEMENT 2021

A SYSTEM FOR VALUE DELIVERY

ASFVD-01 **CREATING VALUE**	ASFVD-02 **GOVERN-ANCE**	ASFVD-03 **PM FUNC-TIONS**	ASFVD-04 **ENVIRON-MENT**	ASFVD-05 **PRODUCT MGMT**
Can best be realized by first satisfying the project goal, an office building, then booster, the world's highest tower status.	Sponsor's strategic input can be key to project success, e.g. Raskob, NYC buy-in, strategy, funding, and operating.	Linear sched-uling can be a great oversight tool to monitor crews' movements and spot issues, e.g. upwards progress of the ESB.	Working in a competition environment can go a long way in achiev-ing greatness, e.g. NYC high rises' Race into the Sky.	Managing benefits beyond completion is key to product success, e.g. ESB was devel-oped, operated then sold w/ high profit mar-gun.yal family.

PROJECT MANAGEMENT PRINCIPLES

PMP-01 **STEWARDSHIP**	PMP-02 **TEAM COLLAB**	PMP-03 **STAKEHOLDERS**	PMP-04 **VALUE**
Having a strong sponsor can ensure strong stewardship e.g. a John Raskob	Competing with other projects fuels team collabora-tion, e.g. Race into the Sky.	Investors are key stakeholder enabling project to exist, e.g. Raskob/Du Pont	Value can rise way after the project completion, e.g. ESB's after WWII till now.
PMP-05 **SYSTEMS THINK-ING**	PMP-06 **LEADERSHIP**	PMP-07 **TAILORING**	PMP-08 **QUALITY**
ESB applied linear scheduling to man-age the interaction of system domains	Selecting the right teams and delega-tion yield superior performance.	Applying Just-in-time approach effectively can yield record breaking results.	Precision is a key quality charac-teristic, e.g. ESB was almost a prefab building.
PMP-09 **COMPLEXITY**	PMP-10 **OPTIMIZE RISK**	PMP-11 **ADAPT/RESIL-IENCE**	PMP-12 **ENABLE CHANGE**
Complexity can be avoided through standardization, e.g. ESB typical floors.	Market intelligence on competitors to win, e.g. ESB observing height of Chrysler.	Challenge crises and turn them into opportunity, e.g. ESB in the recession.	Embrace change if/as required to achieve project goal, e.g. ESB height surge to win.

10.1.4 Chapter 4 Florence Dome, Florence, Italy

PMBOK® Guide 6th Edition Project Management Review, Analysis, and Lessons Learned

> **PROJECT SPONSOR:** Project sponsored by Arte della Lana, Florence's strong and wealthy wool guild. A strong sponsor which ensured strong project funding and political support.

> **PROJECT MANAGER:** The renowned master builder Filippo Brunelleschi, taking charge of all project delivery aspects including design, procurement, and construction.

> **PROJECT TEAM:** Local and regional skilled technicians and laborers of various disciplines working with Brunelleschi motivated by the project's national and spiritual purpose.

 INITIAL   INTERMEDIATE   FINAL

> **KA01 PROJECT INTEGRATION MANAGEMENT**
>
> Project integration benefitted greatly from the master builder approach in which the master builder is responsible for all aspects of the project design, procurement and construction.

PROJECT INITIATION	KA02 SCOPE MGMT	KA03 TIME MGMT	KA04 COST MGMT	PROJECT CLOSING
Project had a strong and quick start; mainly due to the detailed preconstruction planning and methodology during the fierce Opera del Duomo Competition	Project scope was perfectly stable thanks to the very clear scope definition	Project took 16 years to lay 4 million bricks; good pace for precise work	Budget was fairly open as project was national and Florence was quite rich	Project closing witnessed a strong finish; that's very important. Achieved through a few years of intentional focus and construction acceleration.
	KA05 QUALITY MGMT	KA06 HR MGMT	KA07 COMM MGMT	
	A great quality decision was using stone 7 m then light bricks in higher levels	Using Skilled And motivated labor can do wonders as the Duomo team did	Despite project duties, Filippo communicated heavily with Client	
	KA08 RISK MGMT	KA09 PROCMGMT	KA10 STAKEHOLDERS	
	Rival Ghiberti appointed to supervise work; a remarkable RM decision.	The extensive use of local materials made procurement effective	Brunelleschi wouldn't let his rivals and haters affect his focus and resolve	

PMBOK® Guide 7th Edition Project Management Review, Analysis, and Lessons Learned

THE NEW STANDARD FOR PROJECT MANAGEMENT 2021

A SYSTEM FOR VALUE DELIVERY

ASFVD-01 **CREATING VALUE**	ASFVD-02 **GOVERN-ANCE**	ASFVD-03 **PM FUNC-TIONS**	ASFVD-04 **ENVIRON-MENT**	ASFVD-05 **PRODUCT MGMT**
Adding a strategic project to a program can boost value high, e.g. adding Florence dome to cathedral made it a world icon.	A strong project delivery body can be key to project success e.g. the role of Opera del Duomo in decision making and oversight.	The Master Builder model cane be the best way to achieving superior results, e.g. the role of master builder Brunelleschi.	Competitive environment can elevate performance to peak levels, e.g. between Brunelleschi and Ghiberti.	Application of product life cycle approach can be key to ensuring value delivery, e.g. cathedral first then dome decades later.

PROJECT MANAGEMENT PRINCIPLES

PMP-01 **STEWARDSHIP**	PMP-02 **TEAM COLLAB**	PMP-03 **STAKEHOLDERS**	PMP-04 **VALUE**
PM taking full ownership of project is key, e.g. master builder Brunelleschi.	Spiritual project nature can fuel team collaboration, e.g. dome of a cathedral.	Negative stakeholders can be motivators, e.g. role of rival Ghiberti to Brunelleschi.	A facility value can jump as a result of a strategic addition, e.g. dome to cathedral.
PMP-05 **SYSTEMS THINK-ING**	PMP-06 **LEADERSHIP**	PMP-07 **TAILORING**	PMP-08 **QUALITY**
Adding a system component can boost value, e.g. adding dome to cathedral.	A strong technical leadership can be key to success, e.g. by Brunelleschi.	Mock up before prototype can be key to success, e.g. herringbone mockup.	Optimize the use of material quality, e.g. stone to start then lightweight bricks.
PMP-09 **COMPLEXITY**	PMP-10 **OPTIMIZE RISK**	PMP-11 **ADAPT/RESIL-IENCE**	PMP-12 **ENABLE CHANGE**
Complex solutions need be documented; e.g. not done in the case of Il Duomo.	Manage innovation risks, e.g. mockup and supervision/reporting by Ghiberti.	Fight for what you know you can do best, e.g. Brunelleschi's defense of his method.	When it doesn't work look for alternatives, e.g. building dome w/o scaffolding.

10.1.5 Chapter 5 Eiffel Tower, Paris, France

PMBOK® Guide 6th Edition Project Management Review, Analysis, and Lessons Learned

> **PROJECT SPONSOR:** Project sponsored by Gustave Eiffel, the renowned contractor and businessman who had the vision, money, and resolve to make the tower happen.

> **PROJECT MANAGER:** Stephen Sauvestre Architect, Maurice Koechin Structural Engineer, and Jean Compagnon for tower erection. All gurus in similar iron structures, e.g. bridges.

> **PROJECT TEAM:** Skilled engineers, technicians, and laborers from G Eiffel's design-build company Compagnie des Établissements Eiffel working in design, fabrication, and assembly.

INITIAL	INTERMEDIATE	FINAL

> **KA01 PROJECT INTEGRATION MANAGEMENT**
>
> Project integration was key to project success by adopting a life cycle approach including concept approval, political support, design, fabrication, erection, delivery and inauguration.

PROJECT INITIATION	KA02 SCOPE MGMT	KA03 TIME MGMT	KA04 COST MGMT	PROJECT CLOSING
Project began with excavation and construct-ing tower foundation in parallel with the design and fabrication of the tower's first stage ironwork base, thus saving time.	Project scope was perfectly stable thanks to the very clear scope definition	Used intensive fast-tracking of iron fabrication and erection activities	Funded mostly by G Eiffel under a 20-year PPP / BOT-like deal with the Gov	Project started quietly but completion was celebrated at the highest level. Func-tional opening took place without lifts aiming to mark early finish.
	KA05 QUALITY MGMT	KA06 HR MGMT	KA07 COMM MGMT	
	Fabrication done in-house in a company-owned workshop thus best QC	Top talents appointed to lead design, fabrication and construction disciplines	The obvious harmony between team leaders allowed excellent comunication. Despite project duties, Filippo communicated heavily with the Client	
	KA08 RISK MGMT	KA09 PROC MGMT	KA10 STAKEHOLD-ERS	
	Detailed wind analysis used to manage the project's top risk of wind forces	Procuring ironwork from a nearby workshop was key to success	Eiffel did great in managing both positive Gov and negative Opp stakeholders	

PMBOK® Guide 7th Edition Project Management Review, Analysis, and Lessons Learned

THE NEW STANDARD FOR PROJECT MANAGEMENT 2021

A SYSTEM FOR VALUE DELIVERY

ASFVD-01 CREATING VALUE	ASFVD-02 GOVERN- ANCE	ASFVD-03 PM FUNC- TIONS	ASFVD-04 ENVIRON- MENT	ASFVD-05 PRODUCT MGMT
PPP agree- ments can present best value to client and developers alike, e.g. the partial funding 20-year use deal Eiffel had w/French Gov.	The design– build approach can present best governance with all aspects controlled by a single entity, i.e. Eiffel's company.	Fast-tracking of multiple delivery tracks can enable seri- ous schedule shortening, e.g. tower design, build, fabri- cation, and installation.	Negative exter- nal environ- ment including fierce critics can be offset by positive internal envi- ronment and team spirit.	Product life cycle Operation agreements can ensure proper maintenance and upgrade of assets leading to enhanced value.

PROJECT MANAGEMENT PRINCIPLES

PMP-01 STEWARDSHIP	PMP-02 TEAM COLLAB	PMP-03 STAKEHOLDERS	PMP-04 VALUE
Strong steward- ship is crucial in hostile External environment, e.g. Paris critics.	National project nature can fuel team collaboration, e.g. a major Expo event.	Managing political external stakeholders is key, e.g. the Expo tech commission. Brunelles- chi's rival Ghiberti.	Value can develop from unique design or a breakthrough, e.g. world's tallest tower.

PMP-05 SYSTEMS THINKING	PMP-06 LEADERSHIP	PMP-07 TAILORING	PMP-08 QUALITY
Subsystems can be key to functionality, e.g. tower elevators and observation decks.	Leadership can extend from cradle to grave, e.g. G Eiffel from concept to retirement.	Design–Build approach can be key to success of strategic projects, e.g. Eiffel Tower.	In-house fabrication can enable better quality control, e.g. Eiffel's iron factory.

PMP-09 COMPLEXITY	PMP-10 OPTIMIZE RISK	PMP-11 ADAPT/RESIL- IENCE	PMP-12 ENABLE CHANGE
Handling com- plexity requires accuracy; e.g. fabrication of the 3D iron elements.	Breakthroughs require detailed risk analysis, e.g. wind force analysis for wind risk.	Ability to perform under pressure is key, e.g. Paris engi- neers and media.	Project can itself be a change from the norm, e.g. Eiffel Tower design.

10.1.6 Chapter 6 New Al Gourna Village, Luxor, Egypt

PMBOK® Guide Project Management Review, Analysis, and Lessons Learned

---

PROJECT SPONSOR: The Egyptian Department of Antiquities based in Cairo, 520 Km away from site. Although funded the project, it didn't give it the required care so project failed.

PROJECT MANAGER: Hassan Fathy, the master builder and innovative Architect, playing a brilliant technical role, however failed to secure sponsor's political support.

PROJECT TEAM: A small team of construction supervisors overseeing skilled and unskilled local workers, all working under the direct supervision of master builder Hassan Fathy.

INITIAL   INTERMEDIATE   FINAL

KA01 PROJECT INTEGRATION MANAGEMENT

Project integration was managed by Hasan Fathy who controlled all project aspects incl. design, construction, change, stakeholders, procurement, resources, time, quality, and cost.

PROJECT INITIATION	KA02 **SCOPE MGMT**	KA03 **TIME MGMT**	KA04 **COST MGMT**	**PROJECT CLOSING**
Project began w/ pre-engineering and socioeconomic studies, which is good, however, should have included a more formal start with law enforcement involvement.	Project scope was well defined and put into phases matching future growth	Project speeded up during flood seasons when farmers joined construction	The wide use of local materials especially mud enabled ca 50% cost reduction	Project was not closed properly, apart from an effort to verify cost efficiency. Lack of owner's support and interest can lead to projects-failure and rejection.
	KA05 **QUALITY MGMT**	KA06 **HR MGMT**	KA07 **COMM MGMT**	
	Mudbricks were a traditional item so quality was easier to manage	Farmers were trained how to build and were used during idle flood seasons	PM communication with Sponsor was deficient leading to failure	
	KA08 **RISK MGMT**	KA09 **PROC MGMT**	KA10 **STAKEHOLDERS**	
	Project should have predicted risk of villagers refusing to relocate	Procurement done completely locally so ideal for sustainable architecture	PM failed to manage sponsor and external stakeholders, so project failed	

PMBOK® Guide 7th Edition Project Management Review, Analysis, and Lessons Learned

THE NEW STANDARD FOR PROJECT MANAGEMENT 2021

A SYSTEM FOR VALUE DELIVERY

ASFVD-01 CREATING VALUE	ASFVD-02 GOVERN-ANCE	ASFVD-03 PM FUNC-TIONS	ASFVD-04 ENVIRON-MENT	ASFVD-05 PRODUCT MGMT
Value can be created by applying low cost engineering solutions, e.g. gravity ventilation and low cost mudbricks.	Sponsor support is key to project success, even with the best PM, e.g. Al Gourna project failed due to lack of Gov support.	On-the-job training of human resources can be a powerful PM tool, e.g. Al Gourna villagers were trained to build their own houses.	Using local materials is a high value and top environmentally friendly solution, e.g. using local mud in mudbrick buildings.	Training tenants to maintain buildings can add value chiefly in rural areas, e.g. Al Gourna tenants were trained on how to build.

PROJECT MANAGEMENT PRINCIPLES

PMP-01 STEWARDSHIP	PMP-02 TEAM COLLAB	PMP-03 STAKEHOLDERS	PMP-04 VALUE
Strong stewardship can promote innovation, e.g. Hassan Fathy's way.	Building own property can promote team collaboration, e.g. Al Gourna villagers.	Engaging external stakeholders is key to project success, e.g. authorities.	Using local materials and resources reduces cost and raises value, e.g. New Al Gourna.
PMP-05 SYSTEMS THINKING	PMP-06 LEADERSHIP	PMP-07 TAILORING	PMP-08 QUALITY
Value generates from the integration of subsystems, e.g. Gourna Master Plan.	Project leader may be a catalyst of change, e.g. H Fathy leading the villagers.	Project phasing can match actual demand, e.g. Phase 1 only 120 families out 900.	Step by step procedures are key to quality consistency, e.g. brick production.
PMP-09 COMPLEXITY	PMP-10 OPTIMIZE RISK	PMP-11 ADAPT/ RESILIENCE	PMP-12 ENABLE CHANGE
Design–build reduces process complexity; e.g. Fathy master builder way.	Risk avoidance can be best, e.g. locating project site out of the river flood corridor.	You may go ahead with project despite opposition, e.g. Fathy despite residents' opp.	Failure to change can lead to failure, e.g. villagers' refusal to relocate.

10.1.7 Chapter 7 Brooklyn Bridge, New York, USA

PMBOK® Guide Project Management Review, Analysis, and Lessons Learned

---

PROJECT SPONSOR: Project sponsored by NYBBC, a dedicated special purpose vehicle founded to fund and direct the project. Great projects require great support and attention.

PROJECT MANAGER: The Roeblings family, namely master builder John Roebling for design and Washington Roebling for construction assisted by his wife Emily Warren Roebling.

PROJECT TEAM: Technicians and laborers mostly immigrants, suppliers, and subcontractors, all working under the direct supervision of Washington and Emily Roebling.

INITIAL   INTERMEDIATE   FINAL

KA01 PROJECT INTEGRATION MANAGEMENT

Project integration benefitted greatly from the continuation of project leadership started with John Roebling, then Washington Roebling and his strong wife Emily.

PROJECT INITIATION	KA02 SCOPE MGMT	KA03 TIME MGMT	KA04 COST MGMT	PROJECT CLOSING
Project had a strong start since design and construction concepts were developed and detailed by John Roebling and explained to Washington	Project scope was simple and well defined which enabled success	Project time was affected by repeated procurement delays	Early fund enables strong start; bridge cost can be repaid through tolls.	Project completion was celebrated at the highest level including the US president. Washington and Emily did not get enough thanks at the time.
	KA05 QUALITY MGMT	**KA06 HR MGMT**	**KA07 COMM MGMT**	
	Quality issues faced due to appointment of unreliable cable suppliers	Project's risk of work at height resulted in high labors/workers turnover	Pioneered remote project management thru Emily and ill Washington	
	KA08 RISK MGMT	KA09 PROC MGMT	KA10 STAKEHOLD-ERS	
	Innovation can have serious risks, e.g. the pneumatic caisson method	Procurement can be delayed by client; best be managed by contractor	Change of people can be risky, e.g. new trustees almost fired Washington.	

PMBOK® Guide 7th Edition Project Management Review, Analysis, and Lessons Learned

THE NEW STANDARD FOR PROJECT MANAGEMENT 2021

A SYSTEM FOR VALUE DELIVERY

ASFVD-01 CREATING VALUE	ASFVD-02 GOVERN-ANCE	ASFVD-03 PM FUNC-TIONS	ASFVD-04 ENVIRON-MENT	ASFVD-05 PRODUCT MGMT
A simple yet strategic project can boost an entire economy, e.g. Brooklyn Bridge enabled economic surge in NYC and the USA.	Governance by public sector can have adverse effect on value e.g. NYBBC's bad involvement in procurement decisions.	Remote project management can work effectively, yet with expertise and frequent reporting, e.g. Washington assisted by Emily.	Vivid economic environment can yield high value projects, e.g. authorizing Brooklyn Bridge after decades of consideration. abeyance.	Post construc-tion monitoring and mainte-nance are key to maintain value, e.g. NYC's frequent bridge monitoring and inspection.

PROJECT MANAGEMENT PRINCIPLES

PMP-01 STEWARDSHIP	PMP-02 TEAM COLLAB	PMP-03 STAKEHOLDERS	PMP-04 VALUE
The master builder model is the ultimate stewardship scenario, e.g. the Roeblings.	Team collaboration can flourish with collab leadership, e.g. the three Roeblings.	Gaining buy-in of powerful bodies is key to project accep-tance, e.g. NYBBC.	Value can realize at and long after project is complete, e.g. the BB to NYC growth.
PMP-05 SYSTEMS THINKING	PMP-06 LEADERSHIP	PMP-07 TAILORING	PMP-08 QUALITY
Integration of subsystems is key to proper function, e.g. towers, cables, deck.	Effective leadership should be based on full ownership, e.g. by the Roeblings.	Adopting a proven approach can be key, e.g. Roebling previous suspension bridges. families out 900.	On-site testing of materials is crucial, e.g. cables testing before use.
PMP-09 COMPLEXITY	PMP-10 OPTIMIZE RISK	PMP-11 ADAPT/ RESILIENCE	PMP-12 ENABLE CHANGE
High safety factor is used to avoid complex analysis, e.g. valuation of wind impacts.	Risk response can be an interim solution, e.g. small qty of costly cables to keep pace.	Strong leaders exhibit high adaptability and resilience, e.g. Washington's illness.	Innovation is the ultimate form of +ve change, e.g. the BB record span.

10.1.8 *Chapter 8 Crystal Palace, London, UK*

PMBOK® Guide 6th Edition Project Management Review, Analysis, and Lessons Learned

---

PROJECT SPONSOR: Project sponsored by a Royal Commission led by Prince Albertin person, assisted by a Building Committee in charge of delivering the exhibition building project.

PROJECT MANAGER: Joseph Paxton, a strong businessman and inventor of glass houses who was the project's center of expertise and managed design, procurement and construction.

PROJECT TEAM: Specialist technicians and laborers in iron, glass and other trades directed by Charles Fox for Construction with technical control by Joseph Paxton and William Cubitt.

INITIAL | INTERMEDIATE | FINAL

KA01 PROJECT INTEGRATION MANAGEMENT

Project integration benefitted greatly from the Building Committee body which served as the predominant organization integrating efforts and ensuring project success.

PROJECT INITIATION	KA02 SCOPE MGMT	KA03 TIME MGMT	KA04 COST MGMT	PROJECT CLOSING
Project initiation first started with a competitive bidding process then switched to direct hire of Paxton to speed up the process and save project from failing.	Project scope crept due to extra interior decoration requirements	Project time reduced by adopting fast prefabricated systems	Project cost exceeded budget due to scope creep during construction	Project was completed right on schedule and its inauguration celebrated at the highest level of leadership level including Queen Victoria and Princess Albert
	KA05 QUALITY MGMT	KA06 HR MGMT	KA07 COMM MGMT	
	Quality of the works managed through continuous material testing	Project relied on local personnel however seen a relatively high turnover	Project had strong vertical communication from Royal down to project Construction Management through Emily	
	KA08 RISK MGMT	KA09 PROC MGMT	KA10 STAKEHOLDERS	
	Project risk of delay managed through proper procurement strategy	Procurement done using the full capacity of skilled iron and glass suppliers	Upwards by G Eiffel, incl Royal Commission and Building Committee.	

PMBOK® Guide 7th Edition Project Management Review, Analysis, and Lessons Learned

THE NEW STANDARD FOR PROJECT MANAGEMENT 2021

A SYSTEM FOR VALUE DELIVERY

ASFVD-01 CREATING VALUE	ASFVD-02 GOVERNANCE	ASFVD-03 PM FUNCTIONS	ASFVD-04 ENVIRONMENT	ASFVD-05 PRODUCT MGMT
Prefab systems can add value to temporary buildings after serving their purpose, e.g. CP iron and glass modular system.	Turnkey design–build approach can enhance governance and add flexibility to the system, e.g. CP turnkey contract.	Special skill can streamline PM functions and reduce issues and approvals, e.g. Joseph Paxton's glasshouse expertise.	Great projects respect the environment, e.g. CP embraced existing old trees and saved lighting energy during the day.	Product life cycle plans such as relocation and long term use can boost value, e.g. CP relocation and reuse as celebration hall.

PROJECT MANAGEMENT PRINCIPLES

PMP-01 STEWARDSHIP	PMP-02 TEAM COLLAB	PMP-03 STAKEHOLDERS	PMP-04 VALUE
Entrepreneurial approach can boost stewardship, e.g. by Joseph Paxton multifaceted experiences model is the ultimate stewardship scenario, e.g. the Roeblings.	A big common goal seen by the world can boost team collab, e.g. CP hosting Expo.	Backing of client representative is key to project success, e.g. Building Committee	Innovative design can multiple value, e.g. the inventive iron and glass Crystal Palace.
PMP-05 SYSTEMS THINKING	PMP-06 LEADERSHIP	PMP-07 TAILORING	PMP-08 QUALITY
Think about system interfaces, e.g. iron and glass need sealant to be watertight.	Supreme rulers' project leadership can do wonders, e.g. the Queen and Prince.	Project design need to serve the intended purpose, e.g. CP as temporary building.	Quality must meet specific project objectives, e.g. CP interior decoration.
PMP-09 COMPLEXITY	PMP-10 OPTIMIZE RISK	PMP-11 ADAPT/ RESILIENCE	PMP-12 ENABLE CHANGE
Modular building can reduce complexity, e.g. the CP iron and glass modular system.	Risk of delay can be reduced by award to a trusted party, e.g. Cubitt to Paxton.	The ability to perform under pressure is key, e.g. in CP inventing under time pressure.	Change can be the way to meet time and budget, e.g. CP change to iron and glass.

10.1.9 Chapter 9 Taj Mahal, Agra, India

PMBOK® Guide Project Management Review, Analysis, and Lessons Learned

---

PROJECT SPONSOR: Project sponsored by the Mughal Emperor Shah Jahan. The popular Emperor worked closely with the project team, even taking project decisions.

PROJECT MANAGER: The Mughal Architect Ustad Ahmed Lahouri, who created the distinctive mausoleum design and supervised construction until completion.

PROJECT TEAM: A large multidisciplinary team of the best architects, engineers, artists, technicians and skilled labors of the time, mainly Indians, Persians and Ottomans.

INITIAL   INTERMEDIATE   FINAL

KA01 PROJECT INTEGRATION MANAGEMENT

Project integration benefited greatly from the direct involvement of Emperor Shah Jahan and the experience and commitment of master builder Ustad Ahmed Lahouri.

PROJECT INITIATION	KA02 **SCOPE MGMT**	KA03 **TIME MGMT**	KA04 **COST MGMT**	**PROJECT CLOSING**
Project initiation proceeded on five parallel tracks, namely, design, land acquisition, procurement of stone, team mobilization, and building deep foundations.	Project scope was well defined from the outset and proceeded without creep	Project time was open with focus on perfection of the quality of the end product	Project cost was unlimited with project funded from imperial treasures	Project completion and closure took place in two main stages, first the main building works, and second the calligraphy and decoration.
	KA05 **QUALITY MGMT**	KA06 **HR MGMT**	KA07 **COMM MGMT**	
	Quality of the works was managed by top specialists of the various trades	Project relied on local and regional skilled labors as and when needed	Project was compact, so face to face communication was possible	
	KA08 **RISK MGMT**	KA09 **PROC MGMT**	KA10 **STAKEHOLD-ERS**	
	Project risk of settlement was managed by using deep foundations	Procurement done proactively using selected sources of best material	Project was human and imperial so stakeholders were positive	

PMBOK® Guide 7th Edition Project Management Review, Analysis, and Lessons Learned

THE NEW STANDARD FOR PROJECT MANAGEMENT 2021

A SYSTEM FOR VALUE DELIVERY				
ASFVD-01 **CREATING VALUE**	ASFVD-02 **GOVERN-ANCE**	ASFVD-03 **PM FUNC-TIONS**	ASFVD-04 **ENVIRON-MENT**	ASFVD-05 **PRODUCT MGMT**
Certain types of projects set aesthetics over cost, so value becomes subjective, e.g. TMM focus was on excellence.	A knowledge-able and highly interested client can take charge of decision making and governance, e.g. TMM Emperor.	Great projects usually have a mastermind for oversight and coordination, e.g. TMM Architect Ustad Ahmed Lahouri. expertise.	Combined moral and national projects can fuel positive environment, e.g. TMM presented by Emperor to his beloved wife. lighting energy during the day.	Durable and low mainte-nance building design can add great value to projects in the long term, e.g. TMM's sturdy design.

PROJECT MANAGEMENT PRINCIPLES			
PMP-01 **STEWARDSHIP**	PMP-02 **TEAM COLLAB**	PMP-03 **STAKEHOLDERS**	PMP-04 **VALUE**
Duty of care is a key stewardship function, e.g. identifying the bldg. settlement risk.	High profile projects can enhance team collaboration, e.g. TMM as royal project.	In highly aesthetic projects, client engagement is crucial, e.g. Shah Jahan. EMPEROR-Building Committee	Value can be more than just worth vs cost, e.g. TMM meaning and charm.
PMP-05 **SYSTEMS THINK-ING**	PMP-06 **LEADERSHIP**	PMP-07 **TAILORING**	PMP-08 **QUALITY**
Project systems can be types of art, e.g. marbles, decoration, and calligraphy. decorations, xxx.	Leadership can take the form of strong and clear vision, e.g. by Emp Shah Jahan Queen and Prince.	Finish-Validate-Start can be the best approach for aesthetic projects, e.g. TMM.	Quality can be best guaranteed by top notch trade masters, e.g. TMM.
PMP-09 **COMPLEXITY**	PMP-10 **OPTIMIZE RISK**	PMP-11 **ADAPT/RESIL-IENCE**	PMP-12 **ENABLE CHANGE**
Symmetrical design can reduce complexity signifi-cantly, e.g. TMM symmetrical design.	Concept sketches is a risk mitigation tool in highly aesthetical projects, e.g. TMM.	Projects can take a long time to achieve its objectives, e.g. TMM.	Changes can be a continuous process teams, e.g. in TMM trade masters.

10.2 Lessons Learned Using Agile Project Management Model

10.2.1 Introduction

The term Agile, in the context or project management, first came about in the United States back in 2001 AD in a document called "Agile Manifesto" issued by a group of 17 American software developers. The document envisioned a project delivery approach that is based on iterative and progressive elaboration, and introduced 4 values and 12 principles. Although basically meant for software development, the Agile Manifesto gained worldwide acceptance and popularity, and took its way to numerous fields of application, including construction. Agile Manifesto has even influenced the well-established Project Management Institute's PMBOK® Guide and the Agile Manifesto way can be clearly traced in the Standard for Project Management introduced in PBMOK Guide 7th Edition discussed in the previous section. According to Dr. Anantatmula and Dr. Kloppenborg in their book "Be Agile Do Agile," agility is the ability to move quickly and easily responding to changing customer desires [Anantatmula and Kloppenborg 2021].

10.2.2 *Chapter 2 Pharaoh Djoser's Step Pyramid, Saqqara, Egypt*

Agile Manifesto Review, Analysis, and Lessons Learned

AGILE ITERATIVE AND PROGRESSIVE ELABORATION NATURE

The project management iterative and progressive nature was evident in two major occasions. The first was with the experimental switch from mudbrick to stone, and, the second with the increase in the pyramid size to meet the client expectation.

AGILE MANIFESTO VALUES

Value-V01 People over Process	Value-V02 Deliver Benefits	Value-V03 Customer Collab	Value-V04 Respond to Change
At the time individuals focus was the norm so applied to the maximum extent	The royal burial room key benefit was delivered early under stage M3	Imhotep was Djoser's vizier so well positioned to ensure his collaboration	Imhotep responded well to pyramid size change between stages P1 and P2

AGILE MANIFESTO PRINCIPLES

Customer-P01 Continuous Delivery	Customer-P02 Welcome Change	Customer-P03 Frequent Delivery	Customer-P04 Daily Interaction
Deliver key benefits followed by secondary, e.g. pyramid first then mortuary functions.	A major change conducted to satisfy client vision, e.g. pyramid major size change.	Project delivered in two stages, first pyramid and second complex.	Imhotep worked closely with Pharaoh and the project team, e.g. a master builder.
Managers-P05 Motivate Team	**Managers-P06** Face-to-Face Mtgs	**Managers-P07** Working Product	**Managers-P08** Constant Pace
Through Spiritual Project Management by having workers work for God	At the time face-to-face meetings were the norm applied to the maximum extent	The pyramid and tunnel functioned and the mortal complex boosted functionality	Progress pace was affected by floods and harvest seasons, otherwise steady. Assessment
Teams-P09 Continuous Excellence	**Teams-P10** Simplicity	**Teams-P11** Self-organizing	**Teams-P12** Continuous Improvement
Imhotep was a polymath and expert in many technical fields including stones	Pyramid stability was ensured by using standard size stones laid at inward angle	The master builder style enabled freedom in team building and self-organizing	Imhotep changed the stone sizes several times for optimization

10.2.3 Chapter 3 The Empire State Building, New York City, USA

Agile Manifesto Review, Analysis, and Lessons Learned

AGILE ITERATIVE AND PROGRESSIVE ELABORATION NATURE
The Empire State Building design concept of had fifteen cycles of change and refinements until approved by Client. The detailed design and construction details were also developed progressively along the construction duration.

AGILE MANIFESTO VALUES			
Value-V01 People over Process	Value-V02 Deliver Benefits	Value-V03 Customer Collab	Value-V04 Respond to Change
The Sky Boys set an example for individuals focus producing greatness	Sometimes only full completion generate benefits, e.g. ESB office bldg.	John Raskob was fully involved in project delivery so fully collaborative	Lamb's response to Raskob's height increase request was swift and exemplary

AGILE MANIFESTO PRINCIPLES			
Customer-P01 Continuous Delivery	Customer-P02 Welcome Change	Customer-P03 Frequent Delivery	Customer-P04 Daily Interaction
Use Just-in-time strategy which is a perfect application of continuous delivery	A major change done to win the race to the sky, e.g. add height to exceed Chrysler.	Delivered in two stages, first major the tower, and second remaining fit outs.	In design–build designer and builder must interact daily, e.g. collocation.
Managers-P05 Motivate Team	Managers-P06 Face-to-Face Mtgs	Managers-P07 Working Product	Managers-P08 Constant Pace
Race to the Sky and tallest building in the world were a great team motivator	Were possible as the client, the designer, and the contractor were NYC based	When completed the building was fully functional and ready to receive tenants	Work proceeded at a constant fast pace w/o any reported halt or acceleration Assessment
Teams-P09 Continuous Excellence	Teams-P10 Simplicity	Teams-P11 Self-organizing	Teams-P12 Continuous Improvement
Obvious in the short construction time with no rework or failure reported	Construction was made simple through wide application of modular systems	The inspiring project mission urged teams to work together and synchronize efforts	Designer worked closely w/ Contractor to improve work

10.2.4 Chapter 4 Florence Dome, Florence, Italy

Agile Manifesto Review, Analysis, and Lessons Learned

AGILE ITERATIVE AND PROGRESSIVE ELABORATION NATURE
The dome construction progressed carefully and in iterative and progressive elaboration manner. That included developing methods for dome setting out, cranes, chains and optimization of the use of materials, e.g. first stone then light weight bricks.

AGILE MANIFESTO VALUES			
Value-V01 People over Process	Value-V02 Deliver Benefits	Value-V03 Customer Collab	Value-V04 Respond to Change
Team was small and highly skilled which enabled good individuals focus.	Delivering a dome even without a Lantern, enabled early benefit delivery.	Brunelleschi involved client all the way from vision to concept to completion	As a master builder, Brunelleschi performed change as and when needed

AGILE MANIFESTO PRINCIPLES			
Customer-P01 Continuous Delivery	Customer-P02 Welcome Change	Customer-P03 Frequent Delivery	Customer-P04 Daily Interaction
Construction went without interruption however with various progress paces	Design optimization is a welcomed change, i.e. from stone to lightweight blocks at higher levels.	Project delivered in two stages, first the dome and second dome lantern.	Daily interaction with client can be made indirectly, e.g. appointing Ghiberti.
Managers-P05 Motivate Team	Managers-P06 Face-to-Face Mtgs	Managers-P07 Working Product	Managers-P08 Constant Pace
Team was greatly motivated by working on a major national house of worship	Team was not large and site was fairly small which enabled face to face mtgs interactions	When completed the dome was fully functional and ready for use by cathedral	Project proceeded at constant pace, slowed down, and then at a faster pace.
Teams-P09 Continuous Excellence	Teams-P10 Simplicity	Teams-P11 Self-organizing	Teams-P12 Continuous Improvement
Brick laying accuracy and creative techniques reached a miraculous level	Dome brick laying work was made simple through a creative setting out system	Brunelleschi orchestrated team efforts in a strong leadership fashion	Evident in the change from stone to brick after 7m height

10.2.5 Chapter 5 Eiffel Tower, Paris, France

Agile Manifesto Review, Analysis, and Lessons Learned

AGILE ITERATIVE AND PROGRESSIVE ELABORATION NATURE

The Eiffel Tower itself was approved by client in one go. However, ironwork fabrication and assembly exemplified such iterative and progressive process where defective ironwork was returned to workshop to be fixed.

AGILE MANIFESTO VALUES

Value-V01 People over Process	Value-V02 Deliver Benefits	Value-V03 Customer Collab	Value-V04 Respond to Change
Project witnessed high people interactions at all levels to exchange information.	Delivering tower even without lifts to the top generated early benefit	Client buy-in was secured at all times despite external opposition	Changes to defective ironwork carried out swiftly to enable continuous erection

---

AGILE MANIFESTO PRINCIPLES

Customer-P01 Continuous Delivery	Customer-P02 Welcome Change	Customer-P03 Frequent Delivery	Customer-P04 Daily Interaction
Continuous delivery was perfectly evident in the ironwork fabrication process obvious construction went without interruption however with various progress paces	Expect resistance to change from negative stakeholders, e.g. critics in Paris.	Fabricated ironwork assemblies delivered to site on continuous delivery basis.	In fast-track projects daily interaction is key, e.g. design, fabrica'n, and erection.
Managers-P05 Motivate Team	**Managers-P06** Face-to-Face Mtgs	**Managers-P07** Working Product	**Managers-P08** Constant Pace
Tallest tower in the world, Revolution and Expo were a great team motivator	Team worked in the same Eiffel Company so face to face meetings were easy	Tower was fully functional and served its purpose as a great World Fair monument	Tight schedule can force constant pace, e.g. ET proceeded at constant pace. throughout due to tight schedule
Teams-P09 Continuous Excellence	**Teams-P10** Simplicity	**Teams-P11** Self-organizing	**Teams-P12** Continuous Improvement
Applied in all tower construction aspects incl. design, fabrication, and erection.	3D elements were not simple, thus occasionally required rework for tuning	G Eiffel cleverly delegated the works to various trusted and capable team leaders	Most team used past projects lessons learned/experiences

10.2.6 Chapter 6 New Al Gourna Village, Luxor, Egypt

Agile Manifesto Review, Analysis, and Lessons Learned

AGILE ITERATIVE AND PROGRESSIVE ELABORATION NATURE

The New Al Gourna Village project followed an iterative and progressive elaboration process in developing mud mixes and training villager to build. Process was also partially applied in getting villagers feedback regarding the new design.

AGILE MANIFESTO VALUES

Value-V01	Value-V02	Value-V03	Value-V04
People over Process	Deliver Benefits	Customer Collab	Respond to Change
Perfectly applied though direct hands-on approach with minimal documentation	Project divided into phases to enable early benefit i.e. phase 1 to enable relocation	Customer was not neither involved nor collaborative thus project failure	No changes reported since project was controlled solely by the Architect

---

AGILE MANIFESTO PRINCIPLES

Customer-P01	Customer-P02	Customer-P03	Customer-P04
Continuous Delivery	Welcome Change	Frequent Delivery	Daily Interaction
Continuous delivery was perfectly evident in the mudbricks fabrication process obvious construction went without interruption however with various progress paces	A concept change should have been effected once refusal was confirmed.	Project delivered in two stages, first houses and second public buildings.	Complete lack of interaction between architect and client can lead to failure.
Managers-P05	Managers-P06	Managers-P07	Managers-P08
Motivate Team	Face-to-Face Mtgs	Working Product	Constant Pace
Hassan Fathy motivated his team vide the promise of mud palaces	Site was so remote that PM did not meet with client f2f leading to project failure	At phase completion buildings were substantially complete and fully functional	Phase 1 construction progress was fairly constant with no recorded stops
Teams-P09	Teams-P10	Teams-P11	Teams-P12
Continuous Excellence	Simplicity	Self-organizing	Continuous Improvement
Through innovative master planning, mud building, ventilation, and sustainability.	Construction used mudbricks which were simple to manufacture by villagers	The Architect led the project team and assigned specific tasks to work crews	Advances in mud construction practices and quality

10.2.7 Chapter 7 Brooklyn Bridge, New York City, USA

Agile Manifesto Review, Analysis, and Lessons Learned

AGILE ITERATIVE AND PROGRESSIVE ELABORATION NATURE
The Brooklyn Bridge development used iterative and progressive elaboration, however through a number of earlier suspension bridges of escalating free spans which were designed and built by John A Roebling at earlier stages.

AGILE MANIFESTO VALUES			
Value-V01 People over Process	Value-V02 Deliver Benefits	Value-V03 Customer Collab	Value-V04 Respond to Change
The site was relatively small so enabled direct individuals focus between staff	Bridge opened to public as early benefit while mass transit system to follow	NYBB Company was collaborated however with spotted negative inputs at times	Washington responded smartly and swiftly to the cables quality issue

AGILE MANIFESTO PRINCIPLES			
Customer-P01 Continuous Delivery	Customer-P02 Welcome Change	Customer-P03 Frequent Delivery	Customer-P04 Daily Interaction
Project used local nearby suppliers and materials to ensure continuous delivery	Change any suppliers or teams once deemed toxic, e.g. a cable supplier.	Project delivered in two stages, first major the bridge, and second mass transit systems.	Daily interaction bet site and management can be done remotely, e.g. Washington-Emily
Managers-P05 Motivate Team	Managers-P06 Face-to-Face Mtgs	Managers-P07 Working Product	Managers-P08 Constant Pace
Team was greatly motivated by working on a public bridge for good payment	Management included constant f2f meetings between Emily and Washington	When completed the bridge was fully functional and ready for use by the public	Progress pace was interrupted by procurement issues causing delays.
Teams-P09 Continuous Excellence	Teams-P10 Simplicity	Teams-P11 Self-organizing	Teams-P12 Continuous Improvement
Spanned the Roeblings design, engineering, construction, and management.	The complex construction feat was simplified using inventive systems	Washington to Emily led and organized team interfaces including suppliers	Inventions of devices for cables extension and spinning

10.2.8 Chapter 8 Crystal Palace, London, UK

Agile Manifesto Review, Analysis, and Lessons Learned

AGILE ITERATIVE AND PROGRESSIVE ELABORATION NATURE
The Crystal Palace iron and glass system including the ridge and furrow roofing took Joseph Paxton years of experimentation and iterative and progressive development to invent before getting used at large scale on the project.

AGILE MANIFESTO VALUES

Value-V01 People over Process	Value-V02 Deliver Benefits	Value-V03 Customer Collab	Value-V04 Respond to Change
Interaction between Joseph Paxton and the Committee was key to project success	In a rare event, moral and marketing benefits began even before opening.	Customer was totally supportive whether Royal Commission or Building Committee	Change management was led by the Building Committee representing client

AGILE MANIFESTO PRINCIPLES

Customer-P01 Continuous Delivery	Customer-P02 Welcome Change	Customer-P03 Frequent Delivery	Customer-P04 Daily Interaction
Continuous flow of supply of iron and glass elements was key to project success	An early change from the norm can lead to great value, e.g. going for glass building.	Project was delivered in full in one go on time for the exhibition.	Daily interaction is a must to manage interfaces, e.g. bet iron and glass works.
Managers-P05 Motivate Team	Managers-P06 Face-to-Face Mtgs	Managers-P07 Working Product	Managers-P08 Constant Pace
Team was greatly motivated working on an innovative and national project	Were key to success incl. the early crisis time f2f meeting bet Cole and Paxton	When completed the Crystal Palace was fully functional and ready for use	Project progressed uninterrupted from start to completion at a constant pace.
Teams-P09 Continuous Excellence	Teams-P10 Simplicity	Teams-P11 Self-organizing	Teams-P12 Continuous Improvement
Building was built simply, accurately, and quickly although an innovation.	Construction was made simple through wide application of modular systems	Iron and glass teams first understood the task then did effective self-organizing	Iron and glass building system developed gradually by J Paxton

10.2.9 Chapter 9 Taj Mahal, Agra, India

Agile Manifesto Review, Analysis, and Lessons Learned

AGILE ITERATIVE AND PROGRESSIVE ELABORATION NATURE

The client, Emperor Shah Jahan, was involved in project implementation, hence design and construction went into cycles of discussions with the Architect, iterative refinement, and progressive elaboration until approved and completed.

AGILE MANIFESTO VALUES

Value-V01 People over Process	Value-V02 Deliver Benefits	Value-V03 Customer Collab	Value-V04 Respond to Change
Site was compact so individuals focus between team members was easy	All mausoleum benefits united and delivered with the full completion	Customer, Emperor ShaJahan, was fully involved in design and implementation	Change was done in real time by the project builders and trade experts

---

AGILE MANIFESTO PRINCIPLES

Customer-P01 Continuous Delivery	Customer-P02 Welcome Change	Customer-P03 Frequent Delivery	Customer-P04 Daily Interaction
Project works proceeded seamlessly from inception to completion	Change can occur in real time during construction, e.g. by trade masters.	Project was delivered in full in one go including full decoration.	Daily interaction can be the Client choice, e.g. told Shah Jahan daily meetings
Managers-P05 Motivate Team	**Managers-P06** Face-to-Face Mtgs	**Managers-P07** Working Product	**Managers-P08** Constant Pace
Team was greatly motivated working on an imperial, unique and noble project	Project site was compact enabling f2f meetings between team members	When completed the Taj Mahal Mausoleum was fully functional and ready for use	Project progressed uninterrupted from start to completion at a constant pace.
Teams-P09 Continuous Excellence	**Teams-P10** Simplicity	**Teams-P11** Self-organizing	**Teams-P12** Continuous Improvement
Quality excellence was the project's first priority over delivery time and cost	Simplicity achieved though the deliberate wide application of symmetricity	Artistic team's self-organization fostered creativity in the decorative works	Done during construction by expert trade masters

10.3 Lessons Learned Using Design–Build Project Management Model

10.3.1 Introduction

Design–build is a project delivery approach in which the owner has a single contract with one entity to provide both design and construction. It is considered a revival of the ancient Master-Builder method, however in modern terms for modern times. The design–build approach is pioneered and promoted by DBIA, or the Design–Build Institute of America (www .dbia.org). As discussed in my book "The Power of Design-Build" [Hashem 2014], design–build project management has two key challenges, namely, selecting the best design–build solution, and fast tracking design and construction activities. To that end, two advanced methods are used, namely, Axiomatic Design and Concurrent Engineering, respectively. Axiomatic design transforms customer needs into best design–build solutions by zigzagging between customer, functional, design, and construction process domains. And, Concurrent Engineering, which is a risk-based method aiming to overlapping design and construction activities safely based on their inherent fast-tracking characteristics.

10.3.2 *Chapter 2 Pharaoh Djoser's Step Pyramid, Saqqara, Egypt*

Design–Build Review, Analysis, and Lessons Learned

First Design–Build Strategy
Axiomatic Selection of Best Design and Construction Solutions

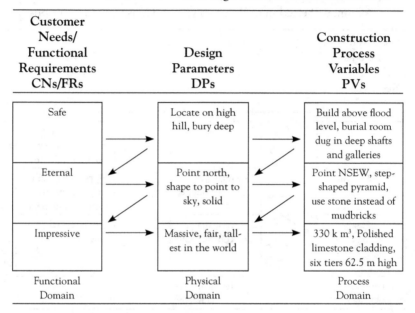

Customer Needs/ Functional Requirements CNs/FRs	Design Parameters DPs	Construction Process Variables PVs
Safe	Locate on high hill, bury deep	Build above flood level, burial room dug in deep shafts and galleries
Eternal	Point north, shape to point to sky, solid	Point NSEW, step-shaped pyramid, use stone instead of mudbricks
Impressive	Massive, fair, tallest in the world	330 k m³, Polished limestone cladding, six tiers 62.5 m high
Functional Domain	Physical Domain	Process Domain

Second Design–Build Strategy
Design and Construction Overlapping/Fast-tracking Strategy

Activity	Timeline
M1 Design M1 Construction	First Design Go – Traditional Stone Mastaba
M2 Design M2 Construction	Second Design Go – Enlarge M1onall four sides
M3 Design M3 Construction	Third Design Go – Enlarge M2 and Install deep shafts
P1 Design P1 Construction	Fourth Design Go – Pyramid 4 tiers
P2 Design P2 Construction	Fifth Design Go – Pyramid 6 tiers w/cladding

10.3.3 Chapter 3 The Empire State Building, New York City, USA

Design–Build Review, Analysis, and Lessons Learned

First Design–Build Strategy
Axiomatic Selection of Best Design and Construction Solutions

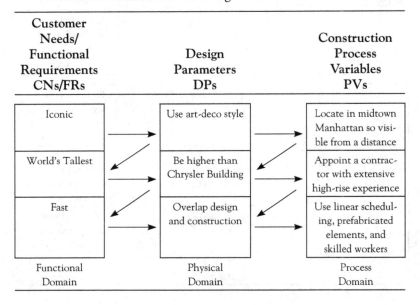

Customer Needs/ Functional Requirements CNs/FRs	Design Parameters DPs	Construction Process Variables PVs
Iconic	Use art-deco style	Locate in midtown Manhattan so visible from a distance
World's Tallest	Be higher than Chrysler Building	Appoint a contractor with extensive high-rise experience
Fast	Overlap design and construction	Use linear scheduling, prefabricated elements, and skilled workers
Functional Domain	Physical Domain	Process Domain

Second Design–Build Strategy
Design and Construction Overlapping/Fast-tracking Strategy

Activity	Timeline [Month Number, Month/Year]
	1 2 3 4 5 6 7 8 9 10 11 12 13 14 15
	2 3 4 5 6 7 8 9 10 11 12 1 2 3 4
	30 30 30 30 30 30 30 30 30 30 30 31 31 31 31

Foundation Design
Foundation Construction   First Design Go

Skeleton Design and Fabrication   Second Design Go
Skeleton Construction

Building/Finishes/MEP Design   Third Go
Building/Finishes/MEP Construction

10.3.4 Chapter 4 Florence Dome, Florence, Italy

Design–Build Review, Analysis, and Lessons Learned

First Design–Build Strategy
Axiomatic Selection of Best Design and Construction Solutions

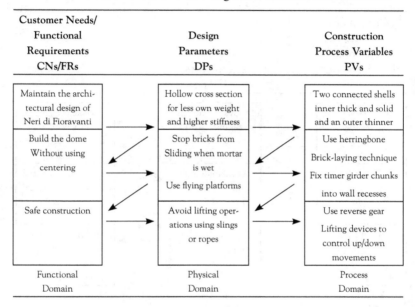

Customer Needs/ Functional Requirements CNs/FRs	Design Parameters DPs	Construction Process Variables PVs
Maintain the architectural design of Neri di Fioravanti	Hollow cross section for less own weight and higher stiffness	Two connected shells inner thick and solid and an outer thinner
Build the dome Without using centering	Stop bricks from Sliding when mortar is wet / Use flying platforms	Use herringbone Brick-laying technique / Fix timer girder chunks into wall recesses
Safe construction	Avoid lifting operations using slings or ropes	Use reverse gear Lifting devices to control up/down movements
Functional Domain	Physical Domain	Process Domain

Second Design–Build Strategy
Design and Construction Overlapping/Fast-tracking Strategy

Activity	Timeline [in Years]
	1 2 3 4 5 6 7 8 9 10 11 12 13 14 15 16
Dome Design	Dome Design and Methodology
Dome Construction	Dome Construction and Finishes

10.3.5 Chapter 5 Eiffel Tower, Paris, France

Design–Build Review, Analysis, and Lessons Learned

First Design–Build Strategy
Axiomatic Selection of Best Design and Construction Solutions

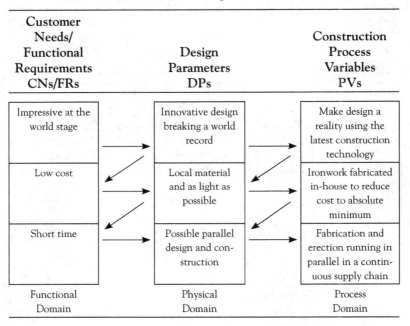

Customer Needs/ Functional Requirements CNs/FRs	Design Parameters DPs	Construction Process Variables PVs
Impressive at the world stage	Innovative design breaking a world record	Make design a reality using the latest construction technology
Low cost	Local material and as light as possible	Ironwork fabricated in-house to reduce cost to absolute minimum
Short time	Possible parallel design and construction	Fabrication and erection running in parallel in a continuous supply chain
Functional Domain	Physical Domain	Process Domain

Second Design–Build Strategy
Design and Construction Overlapping/Fast-tracking Strategy

Activity	Timel ine [in Months]
	2 4 6 8 10 12 14 16 18 20 22 24 26
Design	
Construction – Foundations	
Construction – Iron Fabrication	
Construction – Tower Erection	

10.3.6 Chapter 6 New Al Gourna Village, Luxor, Egypt

Design–Build Review, Analysis, and Lessons Learned

First Design–Build Strategy
Axiomatic Selection of Best Design and Construction Solutions

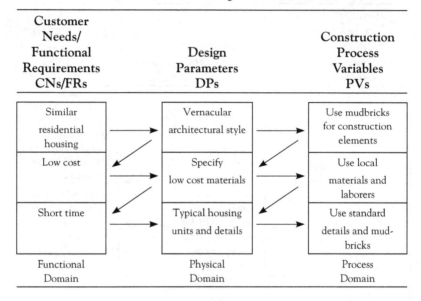

Customer Needs/ Functional Requirements CNs/FRs	Design Parameters DPs	Construction Process Variables PVs
Similar residential housing	Vernacular architectural style	Use mudbricks for construction elements
Low cost	Specify low cost materials	Use local materials and laborers
Short time	Typical housing units and details	Use standard details and mudbricks
Functional Domain	Physical Domain	Process Domain

Second Design–Build Strategy
Design and Construction Overlapping/Fast-tracking Strategy

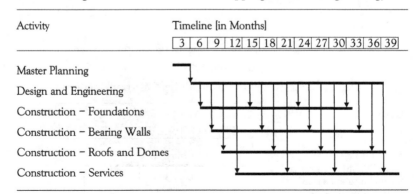

Activity	Timeline [in Months]
	3 | 6 | 9 | 12| 15| 18| 21| 24| 27| 30| 33| 36| 39|
Master Planning	
Design and Engineering	
Construction – Foundations	
Construction – Bearing Walls	
Construction – Roofs and Domes	
Construction – Services	

10.3.7 Chapter 7 Brooklyn Bridge, New York City, USA

Design–Build Review, Analysis, and Lessons Learned

First Design–Build Strategy
Axiomatic Selection of Best Design and Construction Solutions

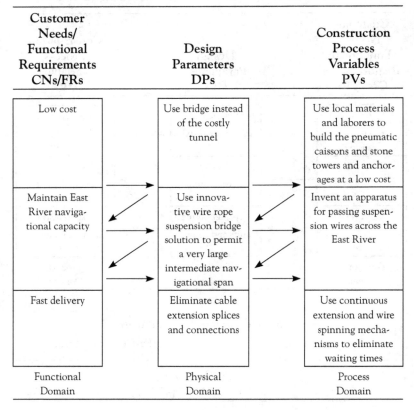

Customer Needs/ Functional Requirements CNs/FRs	Design Parameters DPs	Construction Process Variables PVs
Low cost	Use bridge instead of the costly tunnel	Use local materials and laborers to build the pneumatic caissons and stone towers and anchorages at a low cost
Maintain East River navigational capacity	Use innovative wire rope suspension bridge solution to permit a very large intermediate navigational span	Invent an apparatus for passing suspension wires across the East River
Fast delivery	Eliminate cable extension splices and connections	Use continuous extension and wire spinning mechanisms to eliminate waiting times
Functional Domain	Physical Domain	Process Domain

Second Design–Build Strategy
Design and Construction Overlapping/Fast-tracking Strategy

Activity	Timeline [in Years]
	1 2 3 4 5 6 7 8 9 10 11 12 13 14 15 16
	1867 AD 1883 AD
Bridge Design - Concept by J. A. Roebling and Detailed Design by Washington and Emily W. Roebling	Flow of Design Information
Bridge Construction - Substructure and Superstructure by Washington and Emily W. Roebling	

10.3.8 Chapter 8 Crystal Palace, London, UK

Design–Build Review, Analysis, and Lessons Learned

First Design–Build Strategy
Axiomatic Selection of Best Design and Construction Solutions

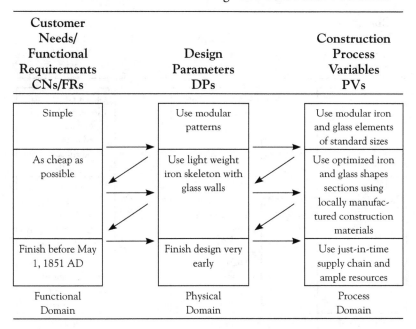

Customer Needs/ Functional Requirements CNs/FRs	Design Parameters DPs	Construction Process Variables PVs
Simple	Use modular patterns	Use modular iron and glass elements of standard sizes
As cheap as possible	Use light weight iron skeleton with glass walls	Use optimized iron and glass shapes sections using locally manufactured construction materials
Finish before May 1, 1851 AD	Finish design very early	Use just-in-time supply chain and ample resources
Functional Domain	Physical Domain	Process Domain

Second Design–Build Strategy
Design and Construction Overlapping/Fast-tracking Strategy

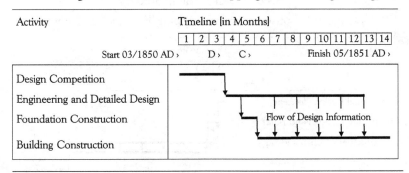

Activity	Timeline [in Months]
	1 2 3 4 5 6 7 8 9 10 11 12 13 14
	Start 03/1850 AD › D › C › Finish 05/1851 AD ›
Design Competition	
Engineering and Detailed Design	
Foundation Construction	Flow of Design Information
Building Construction	

10.3.9 Chapter 9 Taj Mahal, Agra, India

Design–Build Review, Analysis, and Lessons Learned

First Design–Build Strategy
Axiomatic Selection of Best Design and Construction Solutions

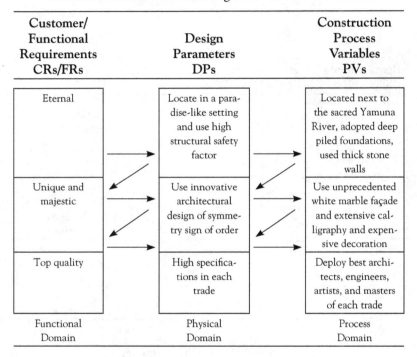

Customer/ Functional Requirements CRs/FRs	Design Parameters DPs	Construction Process Variables PVs
Eternal	Locate in a paradise-like setting and use high structural safety factor	Located next to the sacred Yamuna River, adopted deep piled foundations, used thick stone walls
Unique and majestic	Use innovative architectural design of symmetry sign of order	Use unprecedented white marble façade and extensive calligraphy and expensive decoration
Top quality	High specifications in each trade	Deploy best architects, engineers, artists, and masters of each trade
Functional Domain	Physical Domain	Process Domain

Second Design–Build Strategy
Design and Construction Overlapping/Fast-tracking Strategy

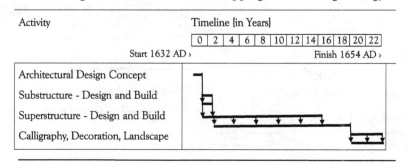

Activity	Timeline [in Years]
	0 2 4 6 8 10 12 14 16 18 20 22
	Start 1632 AD › Finish 1654 AD ›
Architectural Design Concept	
Substructure - Design and Build	
Superstructure - Design and Build	
Calligraphy, Decoration, Landscape	

10.4 Catch-All Project Management Lessons Learned Classified by Project Management Model and School of Thought

This section provides a summary of the lessons learned as observed from all eight great projects together. The listed lessons learned are of holistic nature and not intended to be exhaustive. They are just pulses of wisdom and key findings. More lessons can be extracted by the reader direct while reading the stories, or from detailed tables provided earlier under the first three sections. Lessons learned should be read in conjunction with each other and with the project specific lessons. As always, each project remains unique with own lessons learned and own context and circumstances that need be understood and digested for the full benefit of the presented information.

10.4.1 Top Lessons Learned Using PMBOK® Guide

The PMBOK® Guide 6th Edition and earlier

Lessons Learned Element	Description
Project Sponsor	Great projects require great sponsorship comprising strong both financial and political support.
Project Manager	Great project managers take ownership of projects and act as source of knowledge and expertise.
Project Team	Great project teams are invariably adequate, skilled, and motivated by national and spiritual drives.
Project Initiation	Great projects launch strong and swift starts, best achieved in design–build for the preaward studies.
Project Implementation	Project management must honor the following 10 integrated project management knowledge areas.
1. Project Integration Management	Great projects project integration requires a strong mastermind with a holistic view of project aspects.
2. Project Scope Management	Great projects aim to stability scope through clear scope definition to enable fast steady progress.
3. Project Time Management	Great projects promote fast-tracking of design and construction activities, which is key to fast delivery.
4. Project Cost Management	Great projects are usually funded as needed, with cost reduced by using local material and labor.

(continued)

Lessons Learned Element	Description
5. Project Quality Management	Great projects control quality in each step by trade specialists, and maximize in-house production.
6. Project Human Resources Mgmt.	Great projects engage top talents and highly skilled personnel, and motivate them spiritually.
7. Project Communication Management	Great projects apply effective, close, and continuous communication between all project parties.
8. Project Risk Management	Great projects expect and identify risks proactively and respond to them swiftly and effectively.
9. Project Procurement Management	Great projects use proximate material sources and apply continuous just-in-time procurement.
10. Project Stakeholders Management	Great project leaders can manage key upward and external stakeholders effectively with high focus.
Project Closing	Great projects have strong and client satisfactory finish, accompanied with public celebration.

The PMBOK® Guide 7th Edition (revamped)

Lessons Learned Element	Description
A System for Value Delivery	A system consisting of the following five value delivery concepts and components.
1. Creating Value	Great projects create value in two stages, a basic of function, and a booster of innovative design.
2. Organizational Governance Systems	Governance is usually done by a supreme body that is supporting value delivery, e.g., a royal sponsor.
3. Functions Associated with Projects	Great projects deploy sound planning and multitask fast-tracking orchestrated by the project manager.
4. The Project Environment	Great project leaders interact effectively with the external environment, e.g., politics, critics, media.
5. Product Management Considerations	Great projects realize the product life cycle and take account of sustaining value beyond completion.
Project Management Principles	A system consisting of the following 12 integrated project management principles.
1. Be a Diligent, Respectful, and Caring Steward	Great project leaders take ownership of projects and promote innovation, e.g., master builder style.
2. Create a Collaborative Project Team Environment	Great projects promote team collaboration inspired by moralities, e.g., national pride or spiritual drive.

Lessons Learned Element	Description
3. Effectively Engage with Stakeholders	Great project leaders are great at managing external stakeholders, e.g., authorities, lenders, media.
4. Focus on Value	Great projects generate value through innovative designs and achieving technical breakthroughs.
5. Recognize, Evaluate, and Respond to System Interaction	Great projects integrate subsystems in creative ways and add value by introducing strategic system components.
6. Demonstrate Leadership Behaviors	Great projects leadership is regularly based on trust and motivation, and can be technical or political.
7. Tailor Based on Context	Great project adopt the design–build project delivery approach, besides fast-tracking and standardization.
8. Build Quality Into Process and Deliverables	Great projects use the right material from the right sources and do quality control by trade masters.
9. Navigate Complexity	Great projects avoid complexity, otherwise deal with it using skill, accuracy, and standardization.
10. Optimize Risk Responses	Great projects adopt innovation and manage its risk proactively, e.g., risk avoidance and expert decisions.
11. Embrace Adaptability and Resiliency	Great projects challenge tough conditions, e.g., stone digging, crises, time pressure, or fierce competition.
12. Enable Chance to Achieve the Envisioned Future State	Great projects use change as a strategy to achieve project objectives and they do it as needed.

10.4.2 Top Lessons Learned Using AGILE Manifesto

AGILE Manifesto Nature, Values, and Principles

Lessons Learned Element	Description
Agile Iterative and Progressive Elaboration Nature	Great projects introduce innovation, which requires iterative and progressive elaboration.
Agile Manifesto Values	Four core project management agility values that need be respected and applied.
1. People over Process	Great projects deploy highly skilled talents and focus on motivation and promoting human interactions.

(continued)

Lessons Learned Element	Description
2. Deliver Benefits	Great projects may deliver all benefits at completion, but aim at early, partial, and long-term benefits.
3. Customer Collaboration	Great project leadership includes ensuring customer engagement and collaboration at all times.
4. Respond to Change	Great project leaders respond to major changes personally and swiftly and delegate minor changes.
Agile Manifesto Principles	Twelve core project management agility principles that need be respected and applied.
1. Customer—Continuous Delivery	Great projects apply continuous just-in-time delivery both internally in construction and to clients.
2. Customer—Welcome Change	Great projects use change as opportunity to achieve project goals and to optimize project components.
3. Customer—Frequent Delivery	Great projects deliver major benefits in a first big go at opening, leaving minor works to a second go.
4. Customer—Daily Interaction	Great projects use physical and remote interaction with clients and between individuals and subteams.
5. Managers—Motivate Team	Great projects motivate teams using various reasons including spiritual, national, and prestige.
6. Managers—Face-to-Face Meetings	Great projects realize the importance of human interactions including face to face meetings.
7. Managers—Working Product	Great project leaders strive to deliver early benefits, starting with major functions, then secondary.
8. Managers—Constant Pace	Great projects aim to maximize progress pace and keep it constant unless change or issues happens.
9. Teams—Continuous Excellence	Great project leaders ensure excellence in each step including design, materials, workmanship, and finishes.
10. Teams—Simplicity	Great projects generate simplicity through the use of standardization, symmetry, and modularity.
11. Teams—Self-Organizing	Great projects use Agile self-organizing to reduce process and foster creativity and innovation.
12. Teams—Continuous Improvement	Great projects adopt continuous work improvement within projects and through earlier projects.

10.4.3 Top Lessons Learned Using Design–Build

The Design–Build Project Delivery Approach

Lessons Learned Element	Description
First Design–Build Strategy: Axiomatic Selection of Best Design and Construction Solutions	The first design–build strategy aims to select the best design and construction solutions to implement the project with focus on satisfying the customer requirements in the most effective way.
1. Functional Domain or Customer Functional Requirements	Great projects begin with the accurate and specific determination of customer functional requirements and end product vision and aspirations.
2. Physical Domain or Design Parameters	Great projects use great designers or master builders to turn functional requirements into designs and secure customer approval.
3. Process Domain or Construction Process Variables	Great projects use great builders to turn designs into construction using suitable materials, means, and methods, and deploying top talents.
Second Design–Build Strategy: Design and Construction Overlapping Fast-Tracking Strategy	The second design–build strategy aims to speed up project implementation through safe and controlled overlapping of the project's design and construction activities using concurrent engineering.
1. No to minor structural design and construction breakthrough	Great projects use concurrent engineering in which design and construction proceed in parallel and design information flow into construction.
2. Moderate structural design and construction breakthrough	Great projects use divisive overlapping in which design is divided into packages to be fully completed and validated before release to construction.
3. Major structural design and construction breakthrough	Great projects use the sequential or no overlapping strategy in which design is fully completed and validated before release to construction.

10.5 The Top Ten Secrets of Construction Greatness

A look back at the journey through great projects reveals that construction greatness has certain common traits and conditions precedence. The recurrence of such traits and conditions is likely to bring about again construction greatness. Likewise, achieving construction greatness would require making certain traits and conditions available.

Namely:

1. Great projects are supported by political leadership
2. Great projects are given sufficient funding and resources
3. Greatness can happen under time pressure
4. Greatness goes beyond the state of the art and uses innovation
5. Greatness requires genius minds and uses the design-build method
6. Greatness requires great motivation and great purpose
7. Great projects cause extensive economic and cultural impacts
8. Great projects are necessarily eye-catching
9. Great projects are durable
10. Great projects cannot be copied

Finally, great projects make history and impose new calendars.

Thank You!

References

Chapter 1—The Pathway to Construction Greatness

[1]   Hashem, Sherif 2015. The Power of Design-Build: A Guide to Effective Design-Build Project Delivery Using the SAFEDB-Methodology. ISBN 9781606497708 New York, USA: Business Expert Press. The Power of Design-Build: A Guide to Effective Design-Build Project Delivery Using the SAFEDB-Methodology—Business Expert Press. https://www.businessexpertpress.com/books/power-design-build-guide-effective-design-build-project-delivery-using-safedb-methodology/

Chapter 2—The Step Pyramid

[1]   Tesch, Noah. The Editors of Encyclopedia Britannica. Imhotep Egyptian Architect, Physician, and Statesman. https://www.britannica.com/biography/Imhotep

[2]   Second Dynasty of Egypt 2020. Ancient History Encyclopedia. https://www.ancient.eu/Second_Dynasty_of_Egypt/

[3]   Djoser Photo. Statue de Djéser dans le serdab de son temple funéraire—Saqqarah—IIIe dynastie égyptienne. https://en.wikipedia.org/wiki/Djoser#/media/File:Djoser_statue.jpg

[4]   Imhotep Photo. Imhotep, the ancient Egyptian architect and physician, facts about Imhotep 2020. Egypt Guide. https://www.egyptprivatetourguide.com/egyptian-facts/imhotep-ancient-egypt-architect-physician-facts-imhotep/

[5]   Map of Egypt showing the location of Saqqara https://www.researchgate.net/figure/Map-of-Egypt-showing-the-location-of-Saqqara_fig8_250377712

[6]   Pharaoh Djoser rushing to a popular celebration. https://commons.wikimedia.org/wiki/File:Djoser_running.png

[7]   Bodsworth, Jon 2007. Example of a mastaba. Copyrighted free for use. https://en.wikipedia.org/wiki/Mastaba#/media/File:Mastaba-faraoun-3.jpg https://en.wikipedia.org/wiki/Mastaba

[8]   Typical Mastaba from the Old Kingdom. https://en.wikipedia.org/wiki/Mastaba

[9]   Dunn, Jimmy and Winston, Alan 2020. The Step Pyramid of Djoser at Saqqara in Egypt Part III: The Primary Pyramid Structure Example of a mastaba. http://www.touregypt.net/featurestories/dsteppyramid2.htm

[10]   Rendered View of Djoser Step Pyramid Complex. Discovering Egypt 2020. Step Pyramid at Saqqara. https://discoveringegypt.com/pyramids-temples-of-egypt/step-pyramid-at-saqqara/

[11]   Aerial View of Djoser Step Pyramid Complex. Pinterest. https://www.pinterest.com/pin/239464905157021491/

Chapter 3—The Empire State Building

[1]   Aerial View of The Empire State Building (29 May 2015). Wikipedia Creative Commons. This image is from Unsplash and was published before 5 June 2017 under the Creative Commons CC0 1.0 Universal Public Domain Dedication. https://commons.wikimedia.org/wiki/File:Empire_State_Building_(cropped).jpg
No Copyright. https://creativecommons.org/publicdomain/zero/1.0/

[2]   Headshot of John Jakob Raskob. https://en.wikipedia.org/wiki/John_J._Raskob#/media/File:John_J._Raskob_LOC.jpg

[3]   Headshot of William Emanuel Lamb
https://en.wikipedia.org/wiki/William_F._Lamb
https://www.deviantart.com/rd-dd1843/art/William-Frederick-Lamb-785608849

[4]   Headshot of William Aiken Starrett.
https://en.wikipedia.org/wiki/William_A._Starrett
https://en.m.wikipedia.org/wiki/William_A._Starrett#/media/File%3AWilliam_A_Starrett.jpg

[5]   Aerial view of NYC Lower Manhattan,1924.
https://www.favrify.com/new-york-skyline/

[6]   Reynolds Building in Winston-Salem North Carolina the USA
https://ar.pinterest.com/pin/573083121303467613/

[7]   Initial Architect Sketch of Heights and Allowed Building Areas.
      https://en.wikipedia.org/wiki/Empire_State_Building#/media/
      File:Empire_State_Building_plan.jpg

[8]   Linear Scheduling of Steel Skeleton Design and Construction in
      1930 (excel file available) [13]
      https://leanconstructionblog.com/A-Brief-History-of-Location-
      Based-Scheduling-and-Takt-Time-Planning.html

[9]   Sky Boys: Lunch Atop a Skyscraper
      https://cdn.wallpapersafari.com/67/79/w0VUPy.jpg

[10] The Empire State Building – Under Construction Near Comple-
      tion in 1931
      https://www.thesun.co.uk/living/3456414/empire-state-
      building-construction-workers-photography/

[11] The Empire State Building – Completed Construction in 1931
      https://newyorkerstateofmind.com/tag/al-smith/

[12] The Empire State Building – Completed Construction in 1931
      https://en.wikipedia.org/wiki/Empire_State_Building#/media/
      File:NARA_Empire_State_Building.jpg

Chapter 4—Florence Dome

[1]   Image of Florence Dome
      https://www.florenceinferno.com/wp-content/uploads/2016/09/
      Florence-by-Olatz-eta-Leire-e1474205982394.jpg

[2]   Image of Headshot of Arnolfo di Cambio. Permission granted by
      email from Ruud Teggelaar.
      https://www.teggelaar.com/en/florence-day-3/

[3]   Image of Headshot of Filippo Brunelleschi.
      https://www.britannica.com/biography/Filippo-Brunelleschi

[4]   Image of Headshot of Lorenzo Ghiberti.
      https://en.wikipedia.org/wiki/Lorenzo_Ghiberti#/media/
      File:Ghiberti.png

[5]   3D Drawing of Florence Cathedral without Florence Dome
      National Geographic https://youtu.be/_IOPlGPQPuM

[6]   Image of Brunelleschi defending his egg-shaped effect proposal in
      front of the Opera del Duomo panel.
      https://www.teggelaar.com/florence/imflorence/F9683.jpg

[7]   Image of the DOME Herringbone brick laying model.
https://www.teggelaar.com/en/florence-day-1-continuation-1/

[8]   Image of Headshot of Donato di Niccolò di Betto Bardi.
https://en.wikipedia.org/wiki/Donatello

[9]   Image of Florence dome Cross Section.
http://www.florencedome.com/1/post/2011/06/the-genius-structural-system.html

[10]   Image of 3D Drawing of Herringbone Brick Laying by Francesco Gurrieri 1982.
https://www.mathouriste.eu/Brunelleschi/Brunelleschi-dome-herringbone.JPG

[11]   Image of Stone Lifting Device with Reverse Gear.
https://www.teggelaar.com/en/florence-day-1-continuation-1/

[12]   Image of 3D Graphics of Dome Shells and Hoop Chains.
https://www.teggelaar.com/en/florence-day-1-continuation-1/

[13]   Image of Florence Dome Today By Bruce Stokes on Flickr - [1] CC BY-SA 2.0. https://commons.wikimedia.org/w/index.php?curid=30585923

Chapter 5—The Eiffel Tower

[1]   Image of Eiffel Tower.
https://en.wikipedia.org/wiki/Eiffel_Tower

[2]   Image of Headshot of Gustave Eiffel.
Image Source: https://www.gettyimages.co.uk/detail/news-photo/portrait-of-the-french-engineer-gustave-eiffel-1890s-news-photo/141551141

[3]   Image of Headshot of Maurice Koechlin.
Image Source: https://commons.wikimedia.org/wiki/File:Maurice_koechlin.jpg

[4]   Image of Headshot of Stephen Sauvestre.
Image Source:
https://en.wikipedia.org/wiki/Stephen_Sauvestre#/media/File:Dessin_Stephen_Sauvestre.JPG

[5]   Image of Maurice Koechlin's Sketch of Eiffel Tower.
Image Source:

https://en.wikipedia.org/wiki/Gustave_Eiffel#/media/File:Maurice_koechlin_pylone.jpg

[6] Eiffel Tower General Arrangement and Key Dimensions
Image Source
https://commons.wikimedia.org/wiki/File:Dimensions_Eiffel_Tower.svg

[7] Image of the Proposed Location of Eiffel Tower in Chap de Mars
Image Source: https://en.wikipedia.org/wiki/Eiffel_Tower#/media/File:Les_fondations_de_la_Tour_Eiffel,_ma%C3%A7onneries.jpg

[8] Image of the Eiffel Tower Foundation Overview and Layout.
Image Source: https://sites.google.com/site/engineeringtheeiffeltower/the-eiffel-tower-geotechnical-engineering?tmpl=%2Fsystem%2Fapp%2Ftemplates%2Fprint%2F&showPrintDialog=1

[9] Image of the inauguration of the Eiffel Tower on March 31, 1889
Image Source:
https://artsandculture.google.com/asset/_/KAFC9aHqP17m8w.
Creator Collection Tour Eiffel—licensed under CC Creative Commons.

[10] Image of American soldiers watching the French flag flying on the Eiffel Tower, Ca 25 August 1944. Image Source:
https://en.wikipedia.org/wiki/Eiffel_Tower#/media/File:American_soldiers_watch_as_the_Tricolor_flies_from_the_Eiffel_Tower_again.jpg
[Harvie 2006] Harvie, David I. (2006). Eiffel: The Genius Who Reinvented Himself. Stroud, Gloucestershire: Sutton. ISBN 0-7509-3309-7.

Chapter 6—New Al Gourna Village

[1] The Doomed Domed Mud Palaces of New Al Gourna
Image Source:
New Gourna and Egyptian Architect for Social Justice: Hassan Fathi, 2019. Posted on December 22, 2019 by Miriam Kresh in Architecture, Cities. Link:
https://www.greenprophet.com/2019/12/egyptian-architect-for-social-justice-hassan-fathi/

[2]   Image of Hassan Fathy
      Image Source:
      https://thereaderwiki.com/en/Hassan_Fathy

[3]   Location Map Al Gourna Village, Luxor, Egypt
      Image Source:
      https://www.123rf.com/photo_9072084_illustration-of-egypt-
      map-showing-the-state-borders-.html

[4]   Al Gourna Village, Luxor, Egypt. (Image by: Bernard Gagnon)
      Image Source:
       https://en.wikipedia.org/wiki/File:Gournah.jpg

[5]   The Irregular Urban Planning of Old Al Gourna Village
      Image Source:
      https://www.researchgate.net/figure/The-irregular-urban-form-of-
      Gourna-Source-Authors-and-Google-Earth_fig2_270228310

[6]   Master Plan of New Al Gourna Village by Hassan Fathy
      Image Source:
      http://collectiveimaginaries.org/el-gourna

[7]   Al Gourna Village, Luxor, Egypt (Image by: Bernard Gagnon)
      Image Source:
      https://archnet.org/media_contents/30507

[8]   Green Natural Cooling and Ventilation System
      Image Source:
      https://www.pinterest.com/pin/411375747185760196/

[9]   Al Gournis Training and Then Building their Own New Village
      Image Source:
      Fathy, H. 1973. *Architecture for the Poor: An Experiment in Rural
      Egypt*. The University of Chicago Press, Chicago 60637. The Uni-
      versity of Chicago Press, Ltd., London. © 1973 by The Univer-
      sity of Chicago. All rights reserved. Published 1973. Paperback
      edition 1976. Printed in the United States of America. ISBN:
      0-226-23916-0 (paperbound). Library of Congress Catalog Card
      Number: 72-95133

[10] A Girl Bidding Farewell to Her Old Gourna Home
      Image Source:

Fathy, H. 1973. *Architecture for the Poor: An Experiment in Rural Egypt.* The University of Chicago Press, Chicago 60637. The University of Chicago Press, Ltd., London. © 1973 by The University of Chicago. All rights reserved. Published 1973. Paperback edition 1976. Printed in the United States of America. ISBN: 0-226-23916-0 (paperbound). Library of Congress Catalog Card Number: 72-95133

[11] New Al Gourna—Downtown
Image Source:
Fathy, H. 1973. *Architecture for the Poor: An Experiment in Rural Egypt.* The University of Chicago Press, Chicago 60637. The University of Chicago Press, Ltd., London. © 1973 by The University of Chicago. All rights reserved. Published 1973. Paperback edition 1976. Printed in the United States of America. ISBN: 0-226-23916-0 (paperbound). Library of Congress Catalog Card Number: 72-95133

[12] New Al Gourna—Grand Mosque
Image Source:
Fathy, H. 1973. *Architecture for the Poor: An Experiment in Rural Egypt.* The University of Chicago Press, Chicago 60637. The University of Chicago Press, Ltd., London. © 1973 by The University of Chicago. All rights reserved. Published 1973. Paperback edition 1976. Printed in the United States of America. ISBN: 0-226-23916-0 (paperbound). Library of Congress Catalog Card Number: 72-95133

[13] The Inner Courtyard in a House in New Al Gourna
Image Source:
Fathy, H. 1973. *Architecture for the Poor: An Experiment in Rural Egypt.* The University of Chicago Press, Chicago 60637. The University of Chicago Press, Ltd., London. © 1973 by The University of Chicago. All rights reserved. Published 1973. Paperback edition 1976. Printed in the United States of America. ISBN: 0-226-23916-0 (paperbound). Library of Congress Catalog Card Number: 72-95133

[14]   New Al Gourna Today Encircled by Concrete Buildings
Image Source:
Fathy, H. 1973. *Architecture for the Poor: An Experiment in Rural Egypt*. The University of Chicago Press, Chicago 60637. The University of Chicago Press, Ltd., London. © 1973 by The University of Chicago. All rights reserved. Published 1973. Paperback edition 1976. Printed in the United States of America. ISBN: 0-226-23916-0 (paperbound). Library of Congress Catalog Card Number: 72-95133

Chapter 7—The Brooklyn Bridge

[1]   Image of Brooklyn Bridge—New York, USA
Image Source:
https://en.wikipedia.org/wiki/Brooklyn_Bridge#/media/File:Brooklyn_Bridge_-_New_York_City.jpg

[2]   Image of John Augustus Roebling
Image Source:
https://en.wikipedia.org/wiki/John_A._Roebling#/media/File:Brooklyn_Museum_-_John_Augustus_Roebling.jpg

[3]   Image of Washington John Augustus Roebling
Image Source:
https://www.rpi.edu/about/alumni/inductees/roebling2.html

[4]   Image of Emily Warren Roebling
Image Source:
https://en.wikipedia.org/wiki/Emily_Warren_Roebling#/media/File:Brooklyn_Museum_-_Portrait_of_Emily_Warren_Roebling_-_Charles-%C3%89mile-Auguste_Carolus-Duran.jpg

[5]   Aerial View of NYC 1860s
Image Source:
http://www.old-maps.com/NY/ny-birdseye/0_NYC/NewYorkCity_1865_Bachmann_web.jpg

[6]   Hybrid Suspension and Structural System of Brooklyn Bridge
Image Source:
https://d3i71xaburhd42.cloudfront.net/08dbc6ae2681b-d1eaf6543b216285b65e130e498/8-Figure8-1.png

[7] Pneumatic Caisson Scheme of Brooklyn Bridge
Image Source:
https://www.history.com/news/brooklyn-bridge-construction-deaths

[8] Pneumatic Caisson Workers Brooklyn Bridge
https://en.wikipedia.org/wiki/Brooklyn_Bridge#/media/File:Am-Cyc_Caisson_-_Caisson_of_East_River_Bridge.jpg

[9] East River Bridge Plan of One Tower Designed by John A Roebling
Image Source:
https://tkouloum.wordpress.com/2018/03/21/brooklyn-bridge-schematic-3/

[10] EF Franklin Crossing the East River on a Wire Traveler
Image Source:
https://ephemeralnewyork.wordpress.com/2013/05/23/the-first-man-to-ever-cross-the-brooklyn-bridge/

[11] Walkway, Traveler Wheel, and Suspension Cable System Ready to Start
Image Source:
https://img.piri.net/mnresize/900/-/resim/imagecrop/2020/11/19/06/28/resized_92920-d62806455.jpg

[12] Newspaper Announcement of Brooklyn Bridge Opening
Image Source:
https://en.wikipedia.org/wiki/Brooklyn_Bridge#/media/File:1883_Frank_Leslie's_Illustrated_Newspaper_Brooklyn_Bridge_New_York_City.jpg

[13] Official Popular Celebration of the Brooklyn Bridge Opening
Image Source:
https://en.wikipedia.org/wiki/Brooklyn_Bridge#/media/File:Currier_and_Ives_Brooklyn_Bridge2.jpg

[14] Cross Section of Bridge's Transport Modes and Functions
Image Source:
https://www.structuremag.org/wp-content/uploads/2016/10/1116-hs-4-310x90.jpg

[15] Overview of Brooklyn Bridge from Brooklyn Showing Manhattan 1933 AD
Image Source:

https://2img.net/h/acidcow.com/pics/20120618/from_the_
nyc_05.jpg

[16]   A Recent View of Brooklyn Bridge Central Pedestrian Promenade
Image Source:
https://www.pexels.com/photo/brown-bridge-under-blue-
sky-3318338/
LITERATURE
[NYT, 2018] "New-York; Affairs At The State Capital". The New
York Times. April 18, 2018. ISSN 0362-4331. Retrieved April 23,
2018.
Source: https://en.wikipedia.org/wiki/Brooklyn_Bridge#Planning
[NYT, 2019] "The New York Times. September 11, 1867. ISSN
0362-4331. Retrieved June 21, 2017. Source: https://en.wikipedia
.org/wiki/Brooklyn_Bridge
[Chisholm, 1911] Chisholm, Hugh, ed. (1911). . Encyclopædia
Britannica. 13 (11th ed.). Cambridge University Press. p. 417.

Chapter 8—The Crystal Palace

[1]   Image of The Crystal Place—London, UK
Image Source:
https://en.wikipedia.org/wiki/The_Crystal_Palace#/media/
File:Crystal_Palace.PNG

[2]   Image of Sir Joseph Paxton
Image Source:
https://www.google.com/search?q=joseph+paxton&sxsrf=AL
eKk02xW81UCn7lIZqZNsWmQSWrcqREVA:1613451216386
&tbm=isch&source=iu&ictx=1&fir=kKF97aXXsa74NM%252
CtF0_K8Sx95y5WM%252C%252Fm%252F0yqjm&vet=
1&usg=AI4_-kTdOaQPobTSZJ8J2lVqQvQ8cqdi8w&sa=X-
&ved=2ahUKEwjvufWUzu3uAhWIcn0KHfMrDzkQ_B16BAh-
BEAI#imgrc=kKF97aXXsa74NM

[3]   Image of Sir William Cubitt
Image Source:
https://en.wikipedia.org/wiki/William_Cubitt#/media/File:Wil-
liamCubitt-a.jpg

[4]   Image of Sir Charles Fox
      Image Source:
      https://en.wikipedia.org/wiki/Charles_Fox_(civil_and_railway_
      engineer)#/media/File:SirCharlesFox.JPG

[5]   Joseph Paxton's First Sketch
      Image Source:
      https://archhistdaily.files.wordpress.com/2012/11/paxton.jpg

[6]   Erection of Iron Skeleton
      Image Source:
      https://commons.wikimedia.org/wiki/File:The_Crystal_Palace_
      page_69.jpg

[7]   Erection of Ridge and Furrow Roof System
      Image Source:
      https://commons.wikimedia.org/wiki/File:The_Crystal_Palace_
      page_39.jpg

[8]   Central Glass Transept
      Image Source:
      https://www.pinterest.co.uk/pin/741334788641309455/

[9]   Grand Building Exhibits and Decoration
      Image Source:
      https://www.bl.uk/victorian-britain/articles/the-great-exhibition

[10] The Crystal Palace In Hyde Park for Grand International Exhibi-
      tion of 1851 Image Source:
      https://en.wikipedia.org/wiki/The_Crystal_Palace#/media/
      File:The_Crystal_Palace_in_Hyde_Park_for_Grand_Interna-
      tional_Exhibition_of_1851.jpg

[11] The Crystal Palace After Relocation to Sydenham Hill
      Image Source:
      https://thumbor.thedailymeal.com/40u0QkTFeZqibKYw-
      Z2et8stTIS8=/870x565/https://www.theactivetimes.com/sites/
      default/files/slideshows/106519/109813/17_Crystal_Palace_
      iStock.jpg

[12] The Crystal Palace at Sydenham Hill Set on Fire
      Image Source:
      http://michaelhaag.blogspot.com/2014/11/emile-zola-and-law-
      rence-durrell-in.html

[13]   Queen Victoria of the United Kingdom of Great Britain and Ireland
Image Source:
https://www.imdb.com/name/nm0703075/mediaviewer/rm1237263360/

[14]   Prince Albert of Saxe-Coburg and Gotha
Image Source:
https://upload.wikimedia.org/wikipedia/commons/b/bb/Albert%2C_Prince_Consort_by_JJE_Mayall%2C_1860_crop.png

LITERATURE

[1] White, R.; Yorath, J. (2004). "The Crystal Palace – Demise". The White Files – Architecture. Archived from the original on 28 July 2011. Retrieved 15 June 208. (Quotations from Yorath's original Radio Times article.)

Chapter 9—Taj Mahal Mausoleum

[1]   Image of Taj Mahal
Image Source:
https://cdn.britannica.com/86/170586-050-AB7FEFAE/Taj-Mahal-Agra-India.jpg

[2]   Image of Emperor Shah Jahan
Image Source:
https://www.tajmahal.org.uk/shah-jahan.html

[3]   Image of Empress Mumtaz Mahal
Image Source:
Mumtaz Mahal - Mumtaz Mahal - Wikipedia.

[4]   Image of Ustad Ahmed Lahouri
Image Source:
https://alchetron.com/Ustad-Ahmad-Lahauri#img

[5]   Map of India - Image Source:
https://favpng.com/png_view/united-states-states-and-territories-of-india-madhya-pradesh-rajasthan-united-states-png/8HfxkejZ

[6]   Flag of the Mughal Empire - Image Source:
      https://commons.wikimedia.org/wiki/File:Fictional_flag_of_the_
      Mughal_Empire.svg

[7]   Taj Mahal Elevation Drawing - Step by Step
      Image Source:
      Learn How to Draw Taj Mahal (Wonders of The World) Step by
      Step: Drawing Tutorials (drawingtutorials101.com)
      Taj Mahal Mausoleum - Elevation and Key Dimensions
      Image Source:
      Learn How to Draw Taj Mahal (Wonders of The World) Step by
      Step: Drawing Tutorials (drawingtutorials101.com)

[8]   Taj Mahal Mausoleum – Plan View
      Image Source:
      https://www.wonders-of-the-world.net/Taj-Mahal/Mausole-
      um-of-the-Taj-Mahal.php

[9]   Taj Mahal Mausoleum - Under Construction
      Image Source:
      https://www.aboutcivil.org/sites/default/files/2017-09/taj-ma-
      hal-construction.jpg

[10] Taj Mahal Mausoleum at Completion – Overview
      Image Source:
      https://cdn.dnaindia.com/sites/default/files/styles/full/pub-
      lic/2014/08/18/260264-tajmahalgetty.jpg

[11] Taj Mahal Mausoleum – Gate Calligraphy and Decoration
      Image Source:
      https://www.wonders-of-the-world.net/Taj-Mahal/images/
      Vignettes/Decouvrir/Inscription-lapidaire-V.jpg
      https://www.taj-mahal.net/newtaj/textMM/images/calligraphy8.
      jpg

[12] The Emperor, The Taj Mahal Mausoleum, and The Empress
      Image Source:
      If not Taj Mahal, where was Mumtaz Mahal buried? (theindian-
      ness.com)

Chapter 10—Project Management Lessons Learned

[PMI, 2017] PMI PMBOK® Guide. 2017. A Guide to the Project Management Body of Knowledge—Sixth Edition. ISBN-13: 9781628251845. Project Management Institute, PA/USA www.pmi.org.

[PMI, 2021] PMI PMBOK® Guide. 2021. A Guide to the Project Management Body of Knowledge—Seventh Edition. ISBN-13: 9781628256642. Project Management Institute, PA/USA www.pmi.org.

[Anantatmula/Kloppenborg, 2021] Anantatmula, Dr. Vital S. and Kloppenborg, Dr. Timothy J. 2021. Be Agile Do Agile. ISBN 9781953349941. Business Expert Press, NY/USA www.businessexpertpress.com .

[Hashem, 2015] Hashem, Sherif. 2015. The Power of Design-Build: A Guide to Effective Design-Build Project Delivery Using the SAFEDB-Methodology. ISBN 9781606497708. Business Expert Press, NY/USA www.businessexpertpress.com.

About the Author

Dr. Sherif Hashem is an innovative creative nonfiction writer and a seasoned construction project management guru. His past published work includes *The Power of Design-Build: A Guide to Effective Design-Build Project Delivery Using the SAFEDB-Methodology issued in the United States* by Business Expert Press NY/USA, in addition to numerous holistic project management papers and articles in the United States, Brazil, and the Middle East. Dr. Hashem is a graduate of Alexandria University/Egypt and holder of BSc, MSc, and PhD in Civil Engineering.

Index